Christiana Cawein

Woman and her relations to humanity

Gleams of celestial light on the genesis and development of the body, soul and

spirit

Christiana Cawein

Woman and her relations to humanity
Gleams of celestial light on the genesis and development of the body, soul and spirit

ISBN/EAN: 9783337270216

Printed in Europe, USA, Canada, Australia, Japan

Cover: Foto ©Andreas Hilbeck / pixelio.de

More available books at **www.hansebooks.com**

Christiana Cawein

WOMAN, AND HER RELATIONS TO HUMANITY.

GLEAMS OF CELESTIAL LIGHT

ON

THE GENESIS AND DEVELOPMENT OF THE BODY, SOUL, AND SPIRIT,

AND CONSEQUENT

MORALIZATION OF THE HUMAN FAMILY.

OFFERED ESPECIALLY TO WOMAN FOR STUDY AND CONTEMPLATION; NOT TO THE PHENOMENA HUNTER, BUT TO THE SPIRITUAL STUDENT AND DEEP THINKER.

THE TRUE RELIGION:

MAGNETISM — MATERIALIZATION — REINCARNATION.

DEDICATED

TO

Mrs. Annie C. Cawein,

AS A TRIBUTE OF GRATITUDE FOR VOICING THE
TEACHINGS AND LOVING WORDS

OF THE

"THREE BROTHERS FROM THE MORNING LAND,"

AND OF

OTHER ARISEN FRIENDS OF THE

REPORTER.

WHOEVER was begotten in pure love
And came desired and welcome into life
Is of immaculate conception. He
Whose heart is full of tenderness and truth,
Who loves mankind more than he loves himself,
And cannot find room in his heart for hate,
May be another Christ. We all may be
The saviours of the world, if we believe
In the divinity which dwells in us
And worship it, and nail our grosser selves,
Our tempers, greeds, and our unworthy aims,
Upon the cross. Who giveth love to all,
Pays kindness for unkindness, smiles for frowns,
And lends courage to each fainting heart,
And strengthens hope and scatters joy abroad,
He, too, is a redeemer, Son of God.

ELLA WHEELER.

"If the race ever attains its proper development in earthly life, it must be by knowing and obeying the laws of spiritual evolution. The prenatal conditions must be regarded as of the first importance, and at the starting point of embryonic life, the spirit must have a chance to be embodied aright."— *Communicated by Spirit M. Faraday.*

"Over the unborn, our power is that of God, and our responsibility like his toward us. As we acquit ourselves toward them so let him deal with us."— *Looking Backward, chapter xxv.*

"Man is destined for other and higher spheres. In those spheres or new states of existence, man's spirit must present not only an image and likeness of nature and God, but a consciousness of identity and individual selfhood. Feeling and knowing this, he should so live, while in this rudimentary state of existence, that all his physical, intellectual, moral, and spiritual structure, growth, and maturity, be fully developed, cultivated, and perfected; so that when the 'mortal puts on immortality' and seeks 'a home in the heavens' it can expand into a celestial life without spot or blemish to mar its beauty or impede its progress in bliss and glory eternal."— *From Stellar Key to the Summer Land.*

INTRODUCTION.

THE incidents and conditions which led to the production of the following pages are as follows: In August, 1887, at the close of a private *séance* with the Chicago medium, Mrs. Bishop, her control Red-hand remarked, "Spect you'll have to make a book." — "On what subject?" I inquired. "How to bring papooses into the world and educate them so that their minds won't be tied," was the reply. As I had no literary aspirations, and supposing the Indian used the word make in mistake for write, I gave the thing no further thought, until some two years afterward when in a private *séance* at Louisville, after some twenty-five pages of the book had been communicated to me, I was reminded of the prophecy.

Calling on Wella Anderson, the spirit artist, for a particular likeness, he handed me a sheet of drawing-paper to hold, and, as he said, for me "to magnetize." He left me some ten minutes, returned, laid his watch on the table, tore a jagged corner off of the sheet and retired. Inside of fifteen minutes he returned saying, "I think I have an old Greek here." The jagged corner fitted the torn sheet. Disappointed at not getting the likeness I wanted, yet admiring the head, I was curious to get the name. "Call on the slate-writing medium, Kate Blade," said Anderson, "and you no doubt can get it." After a few hours I was in Mrs. Blade's parlor. She took a clean slate, put a piece of pencil the size of a wheat grain upon it, then placed the slate on the under side of a raised leaf of a breakfast-table, and held it there with her fingers under the slate and thumb on top of the table. Cat never watched a hole for a mouse closer than I did the edge of the slate. The sound of writing, the dotting of i's, the crossing of t's, and finally the sound as if a long pencil had fallen on the slate, was succeeded by Mrs. Blade handing me the slate to read, "He is called Ben Haman and is a very bright spirit." I remarked, "I am impressed that he is a Mahometan." A profusion of raps immediately sounded on the table.

In August '78, sitting with a Louisville writing medium Hofner, Ariosta Bey announced himself: "I am always with you wherever you go. I was a dragoman English consul at Yaddi on the Red Sea. My father was a Greek. . . . I was a young man when I passed over. Allah called me to his bosom. Great honor be to God, Allah the father. I follow your footsteps. There is a great work for you to perform, praise be to Allah. I will follow thee to help thee. We are now three inhabitants who follow you to direct those magic powers only known to the people of the morning land, to work through you, to convince the people there is but one God, Allah the father, who loves all his children, the faithful and the unfaithful, Praise be to Allah."

Ariosta Bey has almost invariably been the first to communicate at every *séance* I have had with the medium through whose organism the body of this work was given. For years he was the chief medical adviser and prescriber of remedies for myself and family whenever any of us were unwell; the medium also received his advice, and followed it with profit.

He also communicated through Horner the following, which, as it seems to be a statement of the object of the subsequent communications of Ben Haman, I introduce here.

I SALUTE you, my friend and brother, in the cause of light and progress. Though it may appear to you at times as if the cause had sunk in apathy, as if a strong undercurrent of indifference had been silently at work, and which, carried by its own force, had made its outburst and deluged the whole visible universe, yet, my friend, I assure you that we, the silent and invisible movers, see and perceive every day more and more the gradual spreading of this grand and beautiful philosophy which is destined to become the beacon light of life, to develop and bring its adherents nearer to the fount of love, the giver of all health bounties.

We have a purpose, an aim in view, in coming down from the celestial spheres to teach mankind their destiny. The lower spheres in spirit life being overcrowded by beings scarcely recognizable as being once the pure, undefiled infant spirit, which once was placed in the fetus in his mother's womb. With pity we receive these monstrosities, pygmies, and crippled souls returning here, who have completely failed in their mission on earth. For each one received a will, a power of discrimination to exercise, to use his own judgment in every station of life. Yet how sadly many have failed to fulfil as they should the work which was assigned to their spiritual capacity.

It is only mind, and nothing but mind, that elevates mankind above the animal creation.

Oh, man! if thou hast received but one talent, put it to usury, do not let it lie dormant and decay. Do not go so far as to deny the assistance of all pervading mind, for thou shalt be called to judgment for all that thou doest and all that thou sayest.

As in the myth days of old, when the immortal Plato dwelt on this plane, no one was admitted under and among his disciples, unless he could claim at least one soul his own in friendship and love. So it should be impressed upon the men living in this country, yourself, your teachers, your masters, and your parents, not to deprive their fellow-men of their rest, not to rob them of the opportunity to develop their spiritual nature in friendly intercourse. Do not draw out existence yourself from the world, but gather round your hearthstone such ones who will satiate this thirsting and famishing from the fountain of life. For it is the grandest, holiest duty, practised both on earth and in heaven, to lift up the fallen, teach the ignorant, heal the suffering, and lead the blind in spirit.

Our aim is to contend against the all enveloping, pervading materialism of those who, grown in error and enmity to God, deny the existence of a personal God, yet secretly, in superstitious fear, worship at the shrine of some dreadful image, and receive for it all power and esteem of their fellows for their self-aggrandizement. We want your co-operation against that hidden form of materialism indulged in by those who vaunt the proud name of Christian, and apparently worship at its shrine. But do their deeds entitle them to bear the holy name of the Godson? Do they follow up his precepts in truth and humility?

Base hypocrisy; and they will be judged accordingly, when their spirits, devoid of this material body, shall display their loathsome hidden deformity. It is for the elevation of the embodied spirit that we descend, that we ask your co-operation. Our motto is, and has been, "Let there be light," which shall pervade every nook and corner, and relieve us from our arduous labor. The human family are groaning under the oppressive influences of a cruel materialism, and perishing from its deadly effects. The time is nigh when the power of an all-pervading love, harmony, and justice shall counteract this anti-christ, shall conquer and crush it never to rise again. Let us, therefore, enlist the assistance of every human soul and teach him and lead him on to victory over his own passions, and by so doing at once *relieve a spirit from his post of duty, to help educate myriads of beings in the lower spheres, who are longing and famishing for one ray of light.* Never tire of helping your friends, as we never tire of doing good. Progression is our watchword, let it be heard everywhere.

ARIOSTA BEY.

Moving to Louisville in the spring of 1879, I shortly afterward called upon and introduced myself to Mrs. Annie Cawein, the instrument used by the dictators of the within communications. At the first or second private *séance*, Benjamin Haman announced himself, and gave me this his first communication which, as he has been the dictator of the major part of this work, I here introduce as an introduction of himself.

"I passed over, not quite two centuries ago, a general in the army of the Persian King, Archibald the Third. My father was a nobleman who lived in Hungary. When the rebellion broke out he fled to Turkey. He disguised himself. I was born in Turkey. I was sent to a military school. Then I went travelling, and remained in Persia; was a friend of the king. He knew my ancestry and gave me a high position. My mother was an Austrian. I took more of my mother than of my father. My mother's maiden name was Elizabeth von Holt, born in Vienna contemporary with Maria Theresa. She married my father against the consent of her father. Mother never saw her relatives after she left. Father held a high position in Turkey. He was involved in the rebellion. He would have lost his head had he remained; but after it was settled he returned to Hungary. I fell in a battle fighting against the Medes, who were a very treacherous people. I left a wife and two children, which caused me to return to earth to benefit them. Consequently, it gave me the knowledge how to control and help humanity. I am attached to you."

He directed me to get a book, he had some communications to make which he wanted me to write down. The commencement was made April 17, 1879. January 26, 1880, a preface was dictated. On June 15 following he urged me to bring out the work, still I delayed. December 23, 1890, I am again urged to "bring it out." "Let us give it to the world. . . . In this little work they will find many rich and rare gems that will assist in spiritualizing the human race."

A word as to the medium. She was given a common school education, and marrying quite young, and raising quite a family of children, her household duties engrossed so much of her time that she could devote but little to reading, and that little was given to novels. When recovering from trance and attaining her normal state, she knew not a single word or thought her lips had uttered while under control. She was an utter stranger to all of my previous life, yet Ben Haman, in control said, "It was my magnetism which restored your spirit to its body when in your youth you fell from the tree." In 1836 I was up a tree after a squirrel, and fell some twenty feet therefrom headlong, my shoulders striking a rail on the ground saved my neck. I lay unconscious from two until five o'clock. His review of my life in his story of reincarnation is wonderfully true. The events alluded to therein occurred in Pennsylvania before the medium was born.

The transmitters of the within communications generally waited until I had written down a sentence before giving a second. Sometimes I was greatly hurried, and in some instances it may be possible I failed to record all the words spoken. However, I tried to be exact. Perfection is not attainable in this lower world. Unless the superior intelligence can find a subject with an organization perfectly adapted to itself, — with a brain intellectually qualified and flexible to its impressions, — the thought attempted to be expressed will be more or less tainted by the idiocrasy of the instrument. According to the plane of development occupied by the reader will he be enabled to comprehend, appreciate, and be benefited by the truths attempted to be unfolded in this little work.

May the gleams of light, falling on creed-bound souls, dissolve the chains which bigotry has forged, and with which it has bound and held them in darkness, and set them free to worship in nature's temple, with no creed but the fatherhood of God and the brotherhood of man, and obtain a realizing sense of their duty in this earthly kindergarten of the soul, wherein they are to prepare for angelic work in the higher life.

REPORTER.

PREFACE.

By Ben Haman, the Spirit Dictator.

January, 1880.

THIS little work is not for the beginner, nor for the phenomenist; it is for the Spiritual student. He who is advanced in the philosophy will be largely benefited by it. So will the deep thinker. Those who are educated on a material plane, who are gifted with the perceptiveness to comprehend, — they too will be largely benefited by its perusal.

To women especially do we offer this work for study and contemplation. She upon whom so much depends, to woman who takes the largest part in reproduction, to whom such great responsibilities are intrusted. She little realizes in youth, or even at a matured age, the great responsibilities which rest upon her and which she is called upon as a creator to fulfil with more perfection.

Man depends upon woman entirely for development. If the organs of reproduction are not regularly formed the offspring cannot develop in Spiritual unfoldment. Woman rocks the cradle, she must learn to comprehend that she also rocks the world.

In this little work which we have offered to humanity, she will have an opportunity of learning what course to pursue in perfecting her offspring, and how she herself can be liberated from the thraldom of sexual slavery. All women who are degraded by an abuse of this law, produce imperfect offspring. No woman should marry under the age of twenty-five years. It is only after she attains a certain period in life that the mind becomes more passive to the natural experiences which, as a matron, should be fully developed.

Too often do we see defects arising from early marriages, — an abuse of sexual relations destroys the nervous system of the mother. No perfect organization can be born from such conditions.

However, we wish to state here that, through a careful perusal of this little work, some germs of knowledge may be attained, and if well applied will assist many who desire to live a perfect life, and who wish to assist in perfecting the human race. It comes to mortals as a germ of peace, laden with good will to mankind, and we repeat again if mothers will perfect themselves, there will be more perfect men born into the world.

June 15, 1880.

BEN HAMAN. — Good-morning, my son! The morning sun shines with its resplendent rays, and illuminates old mother earth with its electric light. So we are again permitted to penetrate earth's magnetism and impart our thoughts to you, which vivifies and electrifies your whole nature.

Yes, my son, we too are grateful for this opportunity, and greatly do we rejoice at being able to manifest our thoughts in words to you this morning, being fully aware of the great need you have of the influence our magnetism imparts, in giving you strength and vitality. True, we can impart it intuitively, which we have lately striven hard to develop. We have exerted ourselves to unfold your faculties, that you may be enabled to comprehend intuitively and perceptively our thoughts as we vibrate them through your sensorium.

The majority of mortals who are intellectually advanced, receive impressions and work them out through their intuitive nature. True, there are many that do not realize whence they come, and give no credence to any power outside of their own mental faculties. Nevertheless, the unseen powers attend them, work with them, and through their instrumentality produce many effects, the experience of which gives them great relief, and they derive much benefit through the accomplishment of any object which brings happiness to the individual or instrument. In this wise, my son, we are working with yourself, hand in hand, my spirit influence guiding your hand many times as well as controlling your mind, and you can now realize why we are so anxious to bring out the little work. Though very simple to us, yet it will make a deep impression on a vast majority of mortal minds. Humanity is in need of such a work; the by-laws of which will give them an insight into the true nature and habits of life in the material form. There has been a great oversight existing in the nature of individuals. They have paid too little attention to the reproduction and proper development of the human race. In fact, we see in many instances where they give more attention in perfecting animals, by crossing them properly, than they do in perfecting the body which is to be the habitation of a soul and spirit.

Our work treats largely upon this subject. The perfecting the human race should accompany the preface of the work. Mortals should strive to comprehend the hygienic laws, in erasing diseases, and establishing a purer element within the system of those who enter upon the sacred duty of reproduction. It is no little thing; and all the suffering, all the sorrow, all the remorse and disappointments, which this life is subjected to at the present day, are the result of imperfect organizations. And just as long as mortals will continue to live on the animal plane, and reproduce offspring through sensual passions, just so long this evil must continue. No perfect organization can be produced through sensual desire and evil designs. This evil must be looked to, and every intelligent mortal man and woman will strive to elevate their offspring, when they comprehend that at the same time they are elevating themselves.

A dutiful son is a pride to a father and mother, a virtuous and loving daughter is an honor to the parents. These can be produced very readily by a strict observation of the spiritual laws attending conception and pregnancy, and it is the duty of all individuals, whether they regard it as such or not, it is their duty to strive and overcome the crude animal propensities which are impregnated in their natures from their progenitors, and to develop into the higher spiritual where they belong. They have assimilated themselves long enough with the animal propensities, it is their duty to strive to attain something higher, that they may overcome this suffering, which they in a true sense bring upon themselves. Ignorance is crime — crime is sin; suffering must follow sin regardless of consequences. Evil brings remorse, remorse is suffering to the spirit.

Regret, which follows any act committed, or any crime perpetrated through ignorance, brings suffering to the individual. None are exempt from it; both young and old share the same fate, for the divine laws work in harmony, and those who sin against them must suffer the consequences. There is no change in those established laws. The Great Infinite mind which constitutes the whole knows no change, but is perfect in its essence and will not permit any one to escape who violates those laws. They attract the aura of that ether which either harmonizes with their nature or is antagonistic.

That ether which harmonizes with the nature of the individual promotes him to happiness and to the enjoyment of all that is spiritual and ennobling to the senses. That which is antagonistic, acts reversely and destroys, is the destructive ether or magnetism. The creative or reproductive is the purer essence, and emanates from the fountain of wisdom and knowledge.

The destructive, in its turn, acts with the same force or power that the creative does. And mortals must learn to discriminate and control alike the good and evil, the productive and the destructive, the positive and the negative. Positive is life, negative is death. And I say unto my fellow-men that by obedience to this law, when studied with careful observation, they can control the prolongation of life.

Those philosophers who lived in the remoter days comprehended the laws more thoroughly than you do at the present day, and many would have lived centuries had not violence interfered. Through ignorance they were destroyed, the ignorance of those who were their superiors in material power.

For this reason, my son, we are striving to impress

upon you the duty of bringing out the work within the reach of those mortals who are intelligent and can comprehend it. Being simple in formation and verb, it will impress upon the mind the necessity of cultivating a purer and more moral nature, and by thus doing they will attract superior influences, and these will impress them with spiritual ideas and develop more spiritual habits.

A spirit never realizes the good work it may have done until it enters the spiritual spheres. Then they realize, as their faculties unfold the reflections from the many, the impressions that are made through the instrumentality of their exertions. This I am acquainted with, and this is why I urge it upon you to bring out the work, which will be a boon to many suffering souls.

I desire to control both your head and hand sometimes. I will impress you to write on subjects of immortality to individuals in the form, and thus you will sow the seed of spiritual knowledge. The impressions which you receive I wish you to take down; and do not hesitate, for your intuitive nature has largely expanded within the last year. I will strive to make it remunerative to you in a material sense, for I fully realize the necessity of material comforts, and now as I invoke a blessing from the all infinite mind upon you, that the all pervading principle may assist us in guiding you aright, that the love and harmony which unites us in spirit may be your guiding star, and that a union of heart and a union of soul may interblend with your spiritual nature, and may ever keep you awake to that conscientious unfoldment of the attributes which interblend with love and power.

We will strive to assist thee, my son, as the father in the material strives to help his offspring. Ay! even more, we will strive to unfold thy faculties of love and honor, which imbeds itself in the sphere of spiritual harmony.

And now may the unfoldment of all thy faculties harmonize itself with our design, and work with us in the accomplishment of this great work. Father of Love, we invoke thy strength. Give us the power and love, with strength to work out the duty towards our fellow-man. May a union of soul interblend our strength, that we may be guided by thy love, oh, father. Amen. B. H.

December 23, 1890.

BEN HAMAN. — I greet you, my son, with happiness.

In going over the work which we gave you years ago, I am very happy to know that everything remains the same. Life is too short, my son, to put off a work of such importance to yourself and humanity. In speaking of yourself, as we have often said before, every mortal has a mission to fulfil. Only a developed mind can realize the importance of doing good. While in the form it is so much easier to accomplish our mission than when out of the form, as we are then not able to control the instruments in the accomplishment of our work. I am only too happy to assist you.

The little work contains gems that will reach minds of a high order that will do good to many mortals. I will state to you that every intelligent mind that works to accomplish its mission, according to its condition, is immortalizing itself, not only in this world, but also in the spiritual world.

Comprehending this as we do, realizing it with such vivid experience, it is our duty to give it to the material world. Look round about you, and see what ignorance is doing, — women destroying their offspring, and men urging it on, — sexual abuse with its deadly influence brought to bear on both sexes. The voice of nature cries against it, and hurls back with damning force, its terrible retribution — ignorant creatures dragged into suffering. Could you see it as we do, the terrors of this evil, you would urge the publication of this little work on with haste, so that we might save, if only a few, by the knowledge its pages contain. Then you and I will feel satisfied that we have done some good for humanity. Spiritual education, enlightenment from above, constitute a sure (preventive) of all this degradation. We cannot impart knowledge without assistance, which must come through spiritualized mediums. I say it is the mediums' heaven-born duty to give their attention to this heaven-born calling. The voice of humanity is crying forth for assistance. Mankind have been drawn down to their lowest depths (of degradation), they must be lifted up out of this terrible condition, they must be drawn nearer to God and heaven.

You observe this wrangling, this jealous contention, one to supersede the other, among religious sects, each one thinking it alone is in the right way, making resolutions and breaking them, laying future plans that are hurled to pieces at their feet, having no power or strength to accomplish that which they most desire, — to attain the knowledge of heavenly things through the religious orders so called. Their foundation is too weak, it has been shaken. The religious creeds have become mouldy and stale. The human race has outgrown them; they are seeking something more in accord with their divine nature. The Divinity within has outgrown their external forms, and is seeking for something in accordance with its own nature.

Now, my son, look over what I have given to be the preface, and I am too happy to grasp the hand of the medium who has helped us in our little work for the benefit of the human race.

Let us give it to the world. Let us strive to do some good. The undeveloped world requires something to lift it out of its degradation. In this little work they will find many rich and rare gems of thought that will assist in spiritualizing the race.

After all is accomplished, and the work is in print, I will set to work to inspire mortals to read it.

CONTENTS.

APRIL 17, 1879. — The liberal spiritual philosophy. The sixth sense. Acquisition of magnetic power develops material and spiritual faculties. Spirit must repeat itself to attain individuality. Individuality necessary to enter the superior spheres. Life is spirit, the outgrowth of the supreme intelligence. The germs of life impregnated in the elements. Disease and plagues caused by atmospheric germs. — *Communication of B. H.* . . . 15

APRIL 18. — It is natural for man to be born again. Jesus a reformer was premature. Was inspired by Moses, Abraham, and Elisha. Spirit must attain identity. Only attained through material magnetism. Reincarnation. Spiritual guides depend upon material magnetism to reveal truth to humanity. — *Communication, from Dr. Wm. Shippen, Otto Watto* 18

MAY 1. — The divine essence of the Creator incarnated in man. Which is spirit indestructible. Manner of incarnation assisted by spirits. Invisibles use the laws of nature to cultivate mortals. The human race deficient in spiritual culture. Consequently unable to receive magnetism from superiors. Man can add to his spiritual nature. Soul and Spirit. The functions of each. Origin of Spirit. External conditions required to unfold it. The grosser the body the weaker the spirit. Spirit requires experiences to unfold its identity. *Communication of Robert D. Owen* 22

MAY 8. — Life, when incarnated. The soul from whence. What it is. Individualized magnetism. The spirit body. Experiences constitute individuality. The more experiences acquired, less number of reincarnations. How to become receptive to impressional power. Acts and thoughts assisted by spirit magnetism. When spirits can control material organs. The spirit

CONTENTS.

power germ the sixth sense. Its development. Effect of gross food. Mind is matter refined. Vegetables and fruit develop spiritual conditions. The happy consequences following the observation and practice of foregoing laws. — *Communication of Father H. S., and Judge Elliot* 31

MAY 15. — The high and holy position of Mother should be comprehended and studied before it is accepted. Few physically or mentally organized to take or comprehend their responsibility. The female should be spiritually cultured. Effect of the mother's mind upon the fetus. The father imparts blood and life, nothing of his spirit. Father responsible for every unkind act. He indirectly affects the fetus. One deficient in organization should not become a parent. — *Otto Watto's Communication* . 35

MAY 22. — Regeneration before generation. The sin of diseased parents. The study of this philosophy gives power to the will to control inherited passions. Effects of a magic circle — of pure and sincere minds upon the sitters, when superior forces assist spiritual development. Spirit grows by acquiring Knowledge. Education. Knowledge and experiences of material life necessary to enter celestial spheres. Knowledge is power, and acts in will-force founded upon love and truth. How acquired. Earthly experiences necessary for spiritual development. Few attain individuality or spirit power. By a repetition of this life man becomes immortalized. Adds and re-adds strength to the perceptiveness of his spiritual faculties. Why many spirits prefer to live on the earth plane. Calamities and disappointments. Means of spiritual development. Why we can tell you of heavenly things which the Nazarene could not. Why man's nature is unfolding faster now than in the past. —*O. W.'s Communication* . . . .

MAY 29. — The new light. Two kinds of magnetism. Man's spirit must be negative to be receptive. When children will be born with intellectual organizations. How the minds of children become impressive to spiritual influences. Spirits the instructors of the present age. Their work. Manual labor causes inertia of mind. Make conditions for spiritual influences. Sacred duty of heads of families to open wide the door for spirit friends. Prayer. Law of spiritual affinity. Families should be reared in the knowledge and practice of the law. When the spirit realizes its true worth. The murderer's spiritual progress. Laws of the body to be observed. Effect of the Nazarene's magnetism while on earth. Mediums receptives of magnetic power. Magnetic power. From whence, and the instrumentality of its transmission — through Circles 43

JUNE 2. — Guardian angels. Two kinds of attending influences. The character of the organization decides the influence attracted. Power of the influences. The pure material magnetism of mediums. Makes conditions for the superior influences to reach the spiritual nature of the erring, which is divine. The development of which germ, good or evil, affected by organization. Mothers give the material body, God the spiritual body. Man and woman should make the laws of organization a study. They should become as one, the same as God and nature. The positive electric and the negative magnetic produce every organized substance, mineral, vegetable, animal, and man. Changes. Law of progression of universal application. — *O. W.'s Communication* 52

JUNE 8. — The germs of life in every thing. Mineral growth. Vegetation. Law of attraction. The sun's rays produce vegetation, minerals, planets, and worlds. All planets contain creative power. No spirit born of mortal has ever discovered from whence this power came. Planets affect each other variously. Atmospheric changes, causes of. The atmosphere a mass of living germs. Acquisition of knowledge develops creative power. God created man in likeness of himself. Man a creator. Through the spiritual philosophy he will learn to perfect the human race. Vegetation not fully developed. Mineral changes in activity and commotion. The atmosphere becoming purified. Reformers, from whence. Powers limited by the organization they occupy. Organizations becoming more perfect, and man more spiritual. Where man stood millions of years ago. Spirit creators. How man enters the new-born life. Takes up in spirit the same character and desires he had on earth. Man and woman should study the laws relating to offspring. The law of attraction. Vegetable, animal, and man developed by cultivation and observance of nature's laws. Education. A knowledge of the laws of God. If man seeks to comprehend them he can live in harmony; living in violation of them he suffers. God does not punish. Man punishes himself 60

JUNE 23. — Sexual intercourse. — The laws of nature prove that God is a father of love. How man becomes formed in his likeness. The three creative laws of life after impregnation. How the mother should employ her mind. Aspiration. Diet. Consequence of observing these laws. Healthy offspring, with organizations flexible to the impressive spirit imbedded for unfoldment. Every thought of the mother impresses the fetus and moulds its character. Parents form the organization, and determine the character of the spirit influence which will be attracted to it. Responsible for the human soul born into life. They build a temple for an angel or a brute. Children should be instructed from the very moment of conception. Kindness of the father to the mother impresses the fetus. Real and true mothers impart to the unborn the beautiful attributes of the psychical organization. Treatment and diet of infants. A change in the infant about the seventh year, when attention should be given to the culture of its mind and spirit — Instruct them how. — *Communication of Judge Edmonds* 72

JUNE 30. — Education of the infant. Education develops in the child the higher attributes of the divine creator. Duty of parents to attend to the spiritual culture of offspring. Instruct them with knowledge. They must develop their own creed — The A B C of the creed should be liberty to man, woman, and child. What children require. Parents should mould their children in the likeness of God. A time should be set apart for spiritual communications when spirit guides may assist. If faithful, parents will receive the power of the holy spirit. The watch over every household. Infant helplessness. Man made dependent upon man. The time when spirit guardianship begins. Results of upward and of downward progression. The soul perishes. Spirit assumes a particular color according to development. Appears as a magnetic light, often reflects itself at *séances*. Relation of soul, body, and spirit. Man and woman an outgrowth of thought. Thought, intellect, knowledge, individuality. Reaction taking place in human progress. Bigotry its effect. The true character of God. The three divine attributes, Love, Hope, and Charity, within the soul, are developed through the natural education which is the liberal spiritual philosophy. 73

JULY 7. — The true Religion. Comparison of the conditions surrounding the old and new reformers. Cause of the liberal

spiritual philosophy now unfolding rapidly. The doctrine of
the immaculate conception understood by few. Chrisna. Parentage of Christ. The mother very mediumistic. Attended
by Elisha, Moses, Socrates, Pythagoras, and a host of others,
developed the fetal organization, and imparted a spiritual nature
to the infant, such as the spiritual band wished for their future
instrument. Christ the incarnation of David the King. His
nature. He advocated the truth of the present spiritual philosophy. He collected to himself a circle of twelve. His psychological power. Its effect upon his disciples. Like a solar
star stood Jesus in the centre. The power and assistance he
gave them. Particulars of the work of Christ's spirit band.
Their selection of a material guardian and instructions to Joseph,
a medium. Guardianship of Mary. Christ educated through
their guidance. They develop his psychological power. The
charge they gave him. The use he made of his power. His
instructions. Character of the Pythagorean philosophy. The
psychological power which Jesus taught the same which the
mediums of the present day are teaching and imparting. The
organs of the medium must be pure. Pythagoras the head of
Christ's spiritual band. Jesus the head of his material band.
Christ's faith in his spiritual band. The true faith needed.
Cause of his views and ideas being misrepresented. The Son of
man will come again. He is in the midst of you all, sustained
by a host of immortals. 82

JULY 14. — The influence of Christ's magnetism on the children of
earth. The new dispensation — its age — what it is — Development. Will-power. Why conflicting ideas are given through
mediums. Why it is essential that mortals should give attention to spiritual things. Jesus, having unfolded his spiritual
power, ascended to do his duty. Seeing the weakness of his
disciples he quickly fulfilled his promises. His directions to
them to sit alone. He imparts the holy spirit. Why they required the magnetism of Christ. The power given the disciples.
They speak in different tongues. This power not understood at
first. Faith in his guardianship led them into the field of duty.
They taught truth as they comprehended it. Reformers not
always comprehended by their hearers. Three or four centuries
afterward the prelates wrote the traditions as they comprehended
them. They did not wish to give conflicting ideas. The cause

of varying sects. All sects branches of the great reformer. He will impart power to all who seek him in sincerity. The great spiritual revolution of the present day. He stands in the centre. Wherever two or three are congregated he imparts magnetic power, the holy spirit. Legions of angels are working out his prophetic words in Europe, America, and the remotest parts of the earth. Christ has worked more faithfully and efficiently than other reformers. Salvation. Experiences of Christ on earth. The outgrowth of his spiritual power. Indefinite conception of the great truth the reformer demonstrated. The great philosophers and remote reformers now in unity with Christ. Buddha. The spiritual philosophy still exists in the Brahma faith. From the central circle in the seventh sphere, where a council is daily held, spirit bands are sent to earth's inhabitants. Impressive ones, or mediums, attract attention from the spiritual universe. The means the reformer is using to draw mankind nearer the great Creator. The sixth sense of man becoming unfolded, and the true philosophy of spiritual life unfolded and comprehended. The world knows little of the inner substance which contains the life-germ. Gradually the spiritual nature of man will unfold and comprehend the true religion of Christ. Children of earth must seek for this knowledge. If they knock at the door assistance will come. They will receive individuality and self-sustenance. Every branch will develop into the spiritual light of the new dispensation. The fatherhood of God and the brotherhood of man the true religion. Where two or three are gathered together he will be in their midst. Salvation of the soul through faith in Jesus Christ. This is the second coming of Jesus Christ. Purify yourselves to hold communion with your sainted ones. Like attracts like 89

SEPTEMBER 23. — Ariosta Bey's criticism of a materialization *séance* 99
Ben Haman's criticism of a materialization *séance*. 101

OCTOBER 10. — Ben H's answer to question, Can fraud ever result in benefiting mortals? 103

OCTOBER 17. — Reincarnation. "Verily I say unto you, except a man be born again he cannot enter the kingdom of heaven." "In my father's house." Many are satisfied with the degrees they have attained on earth. Why Immortals return. Consequence of an imperfect organization. Reincarnation demonstrated by the difference of development. Many in youth superior to those of advanced age. Result of spiritual unfoldment demonstrated by the character. Review of main incidents in the life of the reporter of these communications. A guardian from the moment of material birth. Before this I sought your earthly parentage. Not all guardians can see clearly to choose the more perfect organs for the perfecting of a soul.[1] The spiritual essence is planted in the material essences to encounter experiences, is the law of reincarnation. Man must strive by exertion of his will to control and raise himself above the material. How knowledge is obtained and can be applied to controlling spiritual and material things. To realize that we are all workers for the great central power. I am portraying this divine truth throug assistance of superiors, but doing my duty. I am assisting to perfect our father's children. Story of a spirit's successive reincarnations 108

OCTOBER 31. — Changes in spirit life as well as the material. The magnetic-electric power. Law of their action and results. Man a composition of various elements. When there is a lack of one or more of the elements the body becomes weak, diseased. Oxygen contains the purest electric force. Hydrogen, the magnetic. Their action on the body. Unions in heaven take place, but not as orthodox ministers portray them. The dogmatic error. The doctrine of soul salvation. Why you have so many materialists at the present day. The ignorant are striving to gain their salvation through sectarian creeds. He who always looks upon the dark can never see the light 118

NOVEMBER 14. — Mind and matter. Mind is an essence refined. Of what constituted. The essence of spirit comes in contact with every kind of vegetable and mineral element in the body. The spirit depends upon a healthy body for nourishment and development. Neglect or abuse of the body a sin against the spirit. The study of the law of health a religious, material, and spiritual duty. Mind disembodied is powerful. The soul is material. Electric forces. At death the soul and spirit interblend as one. Then the soul is the spirit envelop. The body develops the soul. Effect of the germ of disease imparted to the fetus. Parents should be healthy and vigorous, and their

---

[1] A guardian often permits undeveloped effects to take place in order to bring out the more perfect and good.

natures opposite. All depends on organization for future progress. Mortals can and have produced Gods. Investigations of the intellectual spirit awaiting reincarnation. Why the best and most intellectual children are often born of poor parents. Who neglect their spiritual duties, and the consequences thereof. Spirits sometimes develop by coming in contact with earth. Spirit friends dine with you many times. The aroma nourishes them. The premature infant brought daily to its mother for magnetism. Guardianship of infants, where and how reared. The maiden's experiences. Infants become guardians. The attributes of the fifth sphere. 124

NOVEMBER 27.— Soul food. Spirit children brought in contact with material magnetism. Youth and adults require the same. The time they require when the body attracts the cruder parts of the electric elements; and the consequences thereof. Law of diet. Gross food injures body, soul, spirit, and intellect. Why cultivate the body. Stimulants. The drunkard drawn back to his fellows goads them on to excesses. Rarely ever a spirit enters spirit-life with a perfect soul. Drawn to Earth to perfect it. Taken in charge by experienced spirits. The soul annihilated, the spirit reincarnates. Will-force, spirit-force. The spirit glorified by the development of will-power. Man makes his own heaven or hades. Charity. Fellowship. Spirit cheer. Spiritual philosophy. The doctrine of spiritual elevation necessary to happiness and contentment. Through the assistance of superior beings the spiritual nature of mortals will unfold. 129

DECEMBER 5.— Recognition of friends in the spirit spheres. The link between mother and child. Spiritual matrons bring spirit children to their material mothers regularly. Few children spiritually allied to their parents. The more parents fulfil their duty, the more spiritual assistance given to them. No restraining force and no dogmatic ideas should be impressed. When this philosophy is understood man will strive to practise the golden rule. Christ tried to initiate the rule. Man not sufficiently advanced to receive it. His magnetism impregnated the soil and atmosphere. Thoughts are potent and convey magnetic power, distance no obstacle. Erroneous sectarian ideas. The Great Creator incarnated in the Saviour! Erroneous ideas undeveloped truth. Magnetism indestructible. Every man leaves a portion of his magnetism in the elements and soil. Bodies as well as spirits require material magnetism. Dispersion of magnetism at death. The human body's origination. Christ's example a lesson to those who denounce Spiritualism. He will come again in the clouds. Mortals striving to reach the truth attract his magnetism. The blood of one atoning for the sins of millions, of the vilest fetishism. This philosophy which Christ strove to develop, brings happy tidings and joyous greetings to weary mortals. Man his own saviour. Strict attention should be given to the growth of the soul, that the spirit may be endowed with power to accomplish noble works in the spiritual spheres. Education and teaching of children. Cleanliness. Godliness. Magnetic power. Will-force 136

DECEMBER 12. — Spiritual children assist their material attraction. Experiences of earth develop large sympathy. They take upon themselves a mission. Its character depends upon the experiences had in the form. Mortals by developing their spiritual faculties can produce any effect they desire. Conception controlled by the will. Sexual intercourse holy and must not be abused. Spiritual nature of father and mother should be cultivated before parentage. Ignorance is sin and the cause of suffering. The harmonious laws of nature not to be trifled with. By cultivation of the spirit, mind becomes powerful. Bonaparte's decisive will. Success in life depends on organic development. 144

JANUARY 2, 1880. — The grosser the food the coarser the development. Simple living on fruit and vegetables develops perceptive and impressional power. A proper care of the body attracts the more developed spiritual power's assistance. Cause of medium's ethereal perceptiveness. Over two-thirds of the human race could become mediums. Where mortals fear to tread angels persist. Angry passions most injurious to the spiritual nature. A passionate nature can be modified by spiritual magnetism. Imparted at every harmonious and sincere *séance*. This philosophy, the true religion of nature, has existed always. Passion and selfishness have retarded its progress. Every nation has formed its own God, and made its own heaven. Not until the true philosophy takes the place of error, will harmony and peace come to earth's children. Scientific development in nature's laws will eventually harmonize and spiritualize man. The spirit body is physical organized electricity. How the electric force purifies the atmosphere. It is also the creative power. . 152

CONTENTS.

JANUARY 9. — The magnetism thrown off from the sun contains creative power. Vegetable, animal, and human life depend upon the electric magnetic rays of the sun. Planets are formed by them. The forces of nature are both negative and positive. The positive electric could not create without the negative magnetic. Why you live and what you live for. The hidden germ. Spiritual teachers now come in large circles to assist mortals. Undeveloped spirits losing power. Faith in spiritual guides, with confidence and sincerity, assists in attaining spiritual knowledge. Laying up material stores a vain folly. Spiritual glory. As the spirit outgrows material desires it becomes more godlike. Gratification of the sensual, destructive to soul and spirit. Sceptics and atheists among the clergy. Their motto. Students of Scriptural philosophy and traditions of undeveloped fungal nations unfit to be teachers. A spiritual teacher must be pure and sincere. A sceptic can make no impression. Conviction a positive force and originates from the creator. Thousands perish like the animal. Their spirit merely exists. They return in fear, dread, and agony which they cannot throw off. They are assisted to incarnate 156

JANUARY 16. — Invocation. Why mortals cling with such tenacity to life. Life exists in all things. Three forms of life. The positive electric combined with the negative creative forces inflate every living substance. Humanity has progressed beyond all other life. Life dependent on the solar rays. Darkness necessary for the unfoldment of the seed in the soil. Vegetable life and death. The law of darkness goes back to the remotest germ of mineral unfoldment. Same conditions required by animal and man. The fish. The serpent and turtle eggs placed in the sun. No deviation from the universal law. Why mortals cling with tenacity to life. The aspiring spirit, by the assistance of its spirit guides, can attain independence. The change by death is but an aspiration to a higher life. The progressive law of individuality. Evil as essential as the good. If there were no sorrow there would be no joy. 161

FEBRUARY 9. — Spiritual essence, what it is. Consequences of realizing that there is a future life. Neglect of the physical body impoverishes the soul. Effect of spiritual knowledge. Spirit-world striving to develop more spiritual teachers to remove the shackles from the slave-bound souls of materialism, and to break the chains of sectarianism. An appeal to the spiritually favored ones, and to fathers and mothers, for assistance. Ignorance develops suffering and is a sin. Remorse erased, how. Individuality required for happiness in future life. The purposes to which wealth should be applied. The heaven-bound duty of the stronger. Consequences of not realizing this duty while on earth. Spiritual sunlight, from whence, and its results. Spiritual knowledge is no belief — is founded upon the sublimest facts, and sustained by the All Infinite. Seek it, oh brother, and angel guardians will assist and protect you. 173

BENJAMIN HAMAN.

By Spirit Artist, Wella Anderson.

WOMAN, AND HER RELATIONS TO HUMANITY.

Communication of Ben Haman.
April 17, 1879.

Your band is very large. We must give your friends opportunity to benefit themselves and you.

THE Liberal Spiritual Philosophy is wide and deep. Many who have investigated understand but a small portion of the truth. God or Deity, in his infinite wisdom, has made laws more perfect than mortals can comprehend. The human race is just emerging out of pagan ideas, pagan forms, and pagan habits.

The development of this science, which is drawn from nature, expands and electrifies the human mind, which is spirit. Spirit is essence divine, and is imparted from Deity, the great fountain of magnetism. Magnetism, so termed, is the life essence of the human body; the cultivation of it is development into the science of the natural laws. Those laws constituting force develop the spirit to comprehend more perfectly how mortals live, and give a true knowledge of God, the infinite creator of all things good and evil.

There is but one power Supreme. Although we have been in spirit-life many centuries we do not yet comprehend that supreme power. We see the beautiful creation, and glory in the magnificence of that all-potent will, creating everything to purify and electrify the senses of every developed spirit.

Through the development of this sixth sense, which is spirit-power to comprehend, we penetrate the potent laws which control spiritual beings, as well as mortals in the material. Through a development of this sense, we discover that there is a law in the elements, which the ordinary human faculties have not discovered (nor can they comprehend it, until the sixth sense, so termed, is developed to a certain standard, to draw in this magnetic power imparted by Nature's laws), which develops the faculties of humanity, and draws them nearer to God, the all-wise, all-loving, and the sublime in purity, and which gives strength both to the material body and spiritual faculties.

This divine law has revealed to us, that the human spirit must repeat itself in different forms, incarnating in different bodies until it obtains individuality. Individuality is a power adhering to the spirit, perfecting it, making it competent to work out through its own individuality the various experiences,[1] which every individualized spirit must seek to obtain. Not until this individuality is acquired, can it enter the superior spheres. You comprehend but vaguely that you have lived before. Your spirit faculties will receive by intuition, and you will learn to comprehend and realize perfectly that you have lived before.

The spirit develops through this magnetic power every faculty that pertains to advancement and perfection. Look about you, see degraded mortals on every side of you!

Since you understand that spiritual power depends upon the development of the faculties in the attainment of knowledge and refinement, in acquiring a power which enables a mortal to work for himself, what spiritual faculties do you suppose they possess? There are none who can attain the faculty, the knowledge of this power in one life, — therefore life must repeat itself.

[1] Experiences. — Instruction and enlightenment. Practical wisdom learned or obtained by the changes and trials of life.

What is life, but spirit? The outgrowth of the supreme intelligence, extending from the spheres beyond, drawing from the fountain of life, the deified attributes of the great fountain of life.

Every plant, every flower, every shrub, will prove to you that reincarnation is a truth. In the first formation of this globe, when all was a vast desert of water, rock, and soil, when vegetation first developed itself, how many thousand years of repetition until the stately oak was developed from a sprig of moss! Then through these various changes, after the oak-tree had spread its branches, and the fig-tree had borne its fruit, how many thousand other years, before a human hand had planted a seed or gathered in the fruits of the soil!

The rivers and vast sea produced the animal development. The germs of life were impregnated through the elements, by nature's laws. Those living germs still inhabit the elements surrounding you. They do not impart the same power now as formerly; there has been a change since the development of the human race. You find living animalcula in the water too numerous to mention. Those living atmospheric germs, impregnating the alcamoles of the water, obtain substance by which they develop and grow. They now frequently impart to the human race diseases and plagues which cause so many to perish; both human beings and animals are daily breathing in those living germs which, coming in contact with certain elementary conditions in their system, readily develop and destroy the physical body.

COMMUNICATION OF DR. WILLIAM SHIPPEN.

April 18, 1879.

Dr. William Shippen, chief medical director of the army under Washington, announced himself.

WELL, S——, Persevere. Keep up a hopeful spirit. All men have their ups and downs in the material form, and you know it. It remains for every one to work out of the crude conditions. It is true that you think you have had experiences, but there are many who have had more bitter experiences than you.

Do you know what this mission has been imposed on you for? To develop your own spirit. God never intended that any one should be idle in this life. Everybody has a mission to fill, and that mission leads to experience. Natural experiences of life are essential to progress. S——, one must learn to be independent. For that we have to learn in spirit-life, if not here. We can only help ourselves by becoming independent. This independence, or self-reliance, individualizes, develops the spirit. When you become independent, the power of your spirit will control those who are with you in spirit. Will-power is a potency only to be cultivated through knowledge.

Confucius comes from a high and holy sphere, his influence is so pure, he can only be felt by a pure mortal. W. S.

Confucius announces himself. "My blessing be upon you, and may the blessing of the divine father always attend you. Bright hopes will give your spirit strength. Your thoughts are but reflections thrown off and taken up by ourselves. After careful analysis of those thoughts, we see what would be good for you and what not. Reflections are the attributes of the spirit and convey to us clear ideas of your spiritual powers. We know then through this observation in what we have to assist you the most. You are yet a pupil. You must attract will-force. Cultivate will-force to attract spirit-force, helping your fellow-man all you can. By always aspiring to truth and spiritual purity you will develop this power which is now unfolding itself within you. Always look on the bright side with a cheerful desire to impart benefit to those who suffer. We have sympathy for our fellow-man, although we are at a great distance from this sphere. Since the great Allah, who created you, created me and all our fellow-brothers, should we not interest ourselves in them, as he does in us? He is all wisdom, all purity, all love. He aids all, both good and evil, without intermission. Both share alike the benefit of his wonderful sympathy, and love and kindness. We should follow the example of his creative power, in giving our assistance to those whom we can benefit, who need more life and light. The darkness which surrounds mankind is so dense, we require material assistance, so that we may benefit them. Be faithful to us, as we are to you. Allah has blessed you in giving you this gift, this power through which we can relieve suffering.

"May the influence of peace, the influence of love, the influence of harmony, abide with you forever and ever, 'till you join us in this beautiful land of brightness, of love, and of sympathy, is Confucius's prayer for his assisting friend and brother. Amen. Peace be with you — good day. C.—"

SECOND COMMUNICATION OF BEN HAMAN.

April, 18, 1879.

WE feel the necessity of this theme. Our thoughts are not idle and vague, but natural and tangible at times, always desirous of making impressions on individuals. We live and love and sympathize with our fellow-man. Knowing and realizing what we have passed through, we deem it our duty to help our material brothers and sisters; so that they may be happier in this life, and not make it a failure, as most of them do, who pass over into the new-born life.

That you have lived before, and that mortals in general have lived before who now live in the form, is an absolute fact founded upon the highest truth; and proves itself, both in spiritual and material life. It is natural for man to be born again to perfect and aid his spiritual progress. It is essential he should pass through various experiences in this life, perfecting his spiritual identity, which he can do by studying this divine philosophy.

Jesus of Nazareth was a reformer. His teachings were not accepted, they were premature, for the human race was just emerging out of that darkness and barbarism in which antiquity committed so much crime. This philosophy was taught by the Nazarene; the fatherhood of God, and the brotherhood of man; but on account of the undeveloped and crude material condition of the human race, men could not accept it. Paganism, so called, predominated in the human mind or spirit. Thirst for blood and revenge for wrong-doing was practised at that day to such an extent, that it almost obliterated the identity of a spiritual being incarnate. A few who gave themselves up to fasting and prayer, could be approached by pure influences in spirit, and be impressed or inspired to speak words of truth and wisdom, encouraging reformation, advising their fellow mortals to live more harmonious and purer lives.

When the Nazarene spoke those burning words of truth, he was inspired by Moses, Abraham, and Elisha. They guided him and communed with him whenever he wished information pertaining to the celestial. They instructed him what course to pursue in order to develop this power and make an impression on mankind; not being successful, his death was premature. It was not ordained by the Divine power, but by the vindictive Romans, who, pagan-like, sought to destroy everything that pertained to refinement, culture, and spiritual progress. What condition or position do you suppose those mortals occupy, after they lay off their material bodies? How much spiritual identity do you presume them to have developed? having lived lives of recklessness and revenge,— undeveloped evil predominating in their whole career — giving all thought to the sensual and the material — paying no attention whatever to spiritual culture; consequently there was no spiritual identity developed. Entering into spiritual life with so little power or strength, there is a natural tendency to downward progress, incarnating in another form, and attaining strength through material magnetism. The spirit seeks to attain its development through material organs, and every wrong must be set aright, and every evil deed must be transformed into some good work, making compensation for that which was omitted in the past life, by working out good effects, accomplishing good works, by assisting to unfold and develop the spiritual nature of yourself and your fellow-man. Ofttimes the spirit must pass through a severe trial, an ordeal of suffering and disappointment, resulting in the development of the faculties. Remember we are depending on material magnetism to reveal this divine truth to humanity. It must and will be accepted, for through this the human race must be purified. Life is not yet understood, nor is it known why you exist at all.

The great Creator has a purpose in creating everything. Forests, fruits, and vegetation are created for the benefit of the human race. Man stands above all; endowed with intellectual and spiritual faculties incarnated with the Divine essence of the Creator, which is spirit indestructible. Consequently, man, being the superior creation, should seek to cultivate the capacities of his organization, the organic life principle of this great power. Spirit, indeed, is Divine essence, and man can become like the Creator, just as much as the son can become like his material father; the material father impregnating the fetus of the unborn babe with natural material habits or inclinations. Just so the spiritual advancement: by exerting the mental capacities through the power of the will, you unfold the spiritual sense, which lies imbedded within the physical organs, and which requires cultivation through and by observation as well as material physical experiences.

That divine essence, or spirit, emanating from the creative power is impregnated through the organs of the female. By inhalation through respiration she imparts the life essence to the fetus, the male giving but the essential portion of liquid essence, which could not impregnate the life if the female respiration did not impart the more essential portion, which is spiritual.   B. H.

At this point I asked a question, which act, Ben Haman said, broke the electric chord of communication. He warned me not to do so again, and requested me to bring the above communication along and read the last part of it at the next sitting.

COMMUNICATION OF R. D. OWEN.

THIS medium little knows what great good she could do, if she paid attention to her controls. Those who have a good medium, and can place confidence in that medium, are blessed mortals in the form.

Friend S——, I see you, too, have a spiritual gift. It is your duty to cultivate it, you owe it to mankind. No one was created to live for himself alone. He should help others; as the great God above helps all, so you should seek to help your brother man.

Mediums are instruments. Just as musical instruments give sound to the magnetic touch of the individual, just so mediums convey expressions to mortals in this material life.

The finer the instrument, the more perfect and refined are the spiritual influences that express themselves through them. A highly strung instrument gives a more perfect tone. So with the medium: the more sensitive, the more spiritual in nature; the purer the habits, the more cultivated and developed are the influences that come within their atmosphere.

Beware of all mediums who are not spiritually natured: if such give themselves up to undeveloped material influences, they cannot impart that satisfaction to the soul or spirit which those who seek the true philosophy of spiritual progress desire. Now, when we look about us, and see so much undeveloped good, we regret that we have not the power of the gods beyond, that we might withdraw from earth and its dark scenes of sorrow and suffering. Still there is a feeling of love and sympathy which impels us to work and assist those who desire to be aided and will receive us, and give attention to our advice and instructions. Yes, we can benefit all who may come within the atmosphere of the medium, who make themselves receptive; we will develop their spiritual sight, that they may see and understand how to work out of their undeveloped condition, by throwing off the crude material and developing the spiritual sense.

Third Communication of Ben Haman.

May 1, 1879.

AFTER reading two or three sentences of the last communication, Ben Haman continued,—The essential portion through respiration is the magnetic electric power, which is the vitality of life. Now the infant is born into the material life with the first respiration of oxygenic atmosphere. The spirit essence divine awaiting in attendance, influenced and assisted by individualized spirits, assimilates itself with this material infant body.

Nature knows no retrogression. It is true, each incarnation is a step toward elevating the spirit, and is therefore designed and ordained by the superior creative power.

Natural laws by observation will reveal to you in every plant, in every shrub, the law of progression to perfection. Take, for instance, the oak-tree of last season. Note the shades of the leaves, also count the branches minutely; and this season make the same observation, and see if there is not a change; the foliage thicker and more splendid in color and hue, a replenishment of the branches, an addition to the trunk, even in root and bark. Take the little wild flower, bring it into your garden, give it attention, place it near some flower of rarity. You will soon see a change of color, the flower becoming fuller and brighter and more perfect. Garden culture improves fruit-trees and vegetation in general with every growth. In a variety of seasons, the vegetation and floral display become more perfect and more beautiful; so it is with the immortal human spirit. Through repetition and change, the crude material which makes the physical body so gross is thrown off, giving the spirit, through physical experiences and through the natural laws of nature, power to progress. When the mind or spirit attains a certain degree of knowledge, it seeks for the superior intellectual knowledge which lies externally all about you. Through the magnetic power the invisibles work and assist in its unfoldment.

Spiritual culture can only be attained through the laws of nature, which the invisibles use as an art to cultivate the spirit incarnate. These spirits incarnated, having had experiences in spirit life, in particle and essence, are one and the same with those who control in spirit. Consequently they can assimilate with each other as acid with alkali.

The human race, viewing it from this present standpoint, lacks in efficiency for want of this spiritual culture. The animal or material propensities predominating both in character and material, the spirit, not having the organic conditions to work through, is unable to receive the magnetic expressions which are constantly imparted from the superior sources. By observing carefully the laws which we are now unfolding to your mental capacities, you will readily observe that you can add much to your spiritual nature.

Admitting that the physical organic life is imparted by the parents, the soul, being that electric magnetic power which adheres to the physical body, needs the assistance of the spirit to cultivate and strengthen it. Authors have frequently united soul and spirit as one principle. They are identically separate as long as they inhabit this earthly body. The soul performs the animal functions to the physical body, which is material organic life. The spirit being the essence divine, emanating from the creative power, has its origin beyond the *vacuo* of space in the interior heavens, unapproachable by spirit perceptions, unless thoroughly individualized and incomprehensible by man; that great creative power, in whose potency are consistent the virtues of love, purity, and power. That essence so potent and divine throws off expressions or thoughts, thoughts which are expressions intellectual. Each thought or each expression contains a life-germ which is spirit. These life-germs incarnated in material bodies constitute the present human race. Now, in the beginning, these expressions are very faint and weak, scarcely perceptible after becoming enveloped in this crude material body, which vegetates and perishes the same as animal and vegetable matter. The spirit requires external conditions to assist it in unfolding the spiritual nature of itself. The grosser the body, the weaker the spirit manifests itself. Consequently it is essential that you should cultivate the physical body, spiritualizing it by strict attention to diet, and habits, and modes of life; never forgetting that the soul takes from the material body certain elements which add strength and purity to the spiritual body, and are essential to its development. For the soul lies folded within the physical body as the butterfly within the chrysalis. If the physical body is carefully nourished the spiritual faculties can work through its organs, assisting its development through its experiences and various unfoldments which are essential to its strength and development. When the spirit attains its development through experience, it unfolds the intellect which the spirit requires, so that it may attain its individuality. Experience in this material life aids the spirit to progress by being informed of natural facts, and unfolding its identity to the great God principle. Very few minds have a conception of how small the first expression thrown off from Deity is. It is but a thought devoid of shape or form, an intellectual thought.

N.B. I have given a higher communication than ever before given to mortal. — B. H.

COMMUNICATION OF CONFUCIUS.

May 1, 1879.

CONFUCIUS. May the great Allah bless you. May he impart this divine essence to you, strengthen you, and preserve you for material spiritual duties.

I come to you, my beloved brother, laden with the fragrance of the spirit-land, desiring to impart it to you and assist you in this noble work toward humanity. We pray that Allah may give us strength and power, wisdom and knowledge, that we may work together in this beautiful truth as two buds within one blossom, diffusing the fragrance of this magnetic emanation over all with whom you may come in contact, imparting love and sympathy and charity to mankind, assisting to unfold their spiritual natures, bringing them nearer to that great fountain of love and knowledge, intertwining their thoughts with the sublimer and purer spiritual beings, developing them in nature to comprehend that they are a part of that divine principle through whom we live and exist.

Now may Allah bless thee, dear and faithful brother, may you ever realize that happiness which Confucius desires to impart to you in perfecting your happiness, by realizing the joys and happiness which you will be enabled to impart to your fellow-man. Allah gives me strength to impart to you, and thy wisdom shall exceed that of others, for you draw it from the fountain of life, that gives you strength to work in the cause of the human race. Blessed be all who receive it through thee; may their eyes be open to the truth divine and the life and the light which lead to true happiness. Amen. Our union is closer now, since me meet more often. Allah bless you. Good-day.

FOURTH COMMUNICATION OF BEN HAMAN.

May 8, 1879.

AN intellectual thought, but not all thoughts are intellectual. This germ contains an intellectual spark, which is life. That spark incarnates the moment the infant draws its first breath in this material atmosphere. The mother imparts the material part, which is magnetism containing life-germs, impregnated through the circulation of her blood, flowing through the placenta to the fetus. Now you have the two distinct life principles, soul and spirit, which are separate in the material body, the soul lying in the material as the butterfly in the chrysalis; every alienation of the soul lying in the physical body, as perceptible as the butterfly in the chrysalis. The chrysalis, passing through certain changes, develops into the butterfly, when nothing but the shell remains. So the soul within the material body. In death the soul, which is individualized magnetism, emerges or withdraws from the material body, gradually concentrating power, and, uniting itself with the spirit, becomes the spirit body. The development of spiritual power gives the soul its reflections in brilliancy or otherwise, according to what it may have acquired in experiences. If through many repetitions the spirit has become individualized, its appearance is of a bright aura. Experiences in the material life constitute individuality. No spirit can become individualized, unless it has repeated experiences of this material life, and those experiences must vary in every branch of knowledge in every mortal. This is not generally understood, and yet it is essential. If the human race could comprehend, they could make many more experiences in a less number of lives.

The influx of this power is a great help in developing the spiritual nature of mankind. It draws them nearer to the spiritual. In giving their thoughts to spiritual things, which are not earthy, they make conditions for their spiritual guides to work upon their mental faculties, developing the sensorium, unfolding that organ, and making it receptive to impressional power. Remember, there is not an act committed nor a thought diffused which is not assisted by spirit magnetism. We control the material organs of this life. When the physical organization is so developed that it is flexible to our influence, our impressions are more readily understood and followed to the benefit of the individual's physical body as well as his spiritual nature.

This spiritual-power-germ belongs to the material body, and is as natural and necessary as the five distinct material senses, which are seeing, hearing, tasting, smelling, and feeling. The sixth sense is the spiritual sense, which reaches out externally, intellectually, and spiritually. It grasps externally from above through the sensorium, working through the magnetic emanations of the material body, and is controlled by the material body as its sustenance depends upon that which the material body takes in for its sustenance and maintenance.

If the body takes in gross material for subsistence, it becomes crude, coarse, and inflexible, developing the material too strong, so that the spirit has very little room to develop and penetrate the inflexible organs.

Mind is matter in a refined state, and is aided by the growth of the physical body; drawing substance from the material body, it in a manner resembles the same. It is, therefore, essential that the human race, should live more on vegetables and fruit, so that this material body develop more spiritual conditions in its emanations. The aura of a drunkard or of a glutton, is dark and murky, the spirit incarnate has no conditions to elevate or expand itself. How essential it is that these truths be taught; were they there would be less suffering and more intelligence developed. The human race would become intellectualized and spiritualized in nature. They would not acquire habits out of impressions made upon the fetus by the parental will.

NOTE.— I want to diffuse this information among the philosophic minded Spiritualists. I wish it understood that the spiritual philosophy must moralize the human race — make them spiritually purer and philosophically more moral . . . gleamings of truths, we may hand down that an infant can comprehend why you give it impressions. B. H.

Communication of H. S.

H. S. (my father) — I must come to say a few words of encouragement to you. Do not let anything interfere with your work. I did not think much of this when on Earth (translated February, 1839). My mind was occupied on a material plane, and did not give much thought to this.

I want you to understand how happy we are that we can communicate. We are drawn to this earth sphere, not for a material purpose, but out of love for my children and their spiritual welfare, which I had not thought of so much when I lived in the physical body. I then looked out for your physical welfare and the physical happiness of all my children. I thought if you all were educated for a profession of some kind, all that duty required, which was essential, was done. True, in one sense of the word. I never dreamed I was neglecting a duty, a serious duty, which I now realize with so much conscientiousness that I am compelled to come and show you the true way, the road to happiness. Through revealing this power to you we are benefiting ourselves. By lightening the burdens of others, we develop ourselves. We give too much (thought) to the material while we live in the material body, too little to the spiritual. I had always striven to be honest with everybody. I never did a dishonorable act to any one, and I was consequently happy. I wanted to come to impress it on my boys, that the temptations of this life are so great that they need spiritual assistance . . . temptations and physical surroundings and influences affect more or less, unless you are strongly guarded by the spiritual influence which you attract.

Rush and Fanny little know how much good they would derive from it if they would give their minds to spiritual communications; life would become a heaven upon earth, if they realized this philosophy.

We will not give anything but the good, the pure, and the elevating.

Communication to Ed.

ED, God is with us in this work. It is the second coming of Christ, the advent. Now that this truth is diffusing itself in the form of magnetism, it can't help but benefit the human race; because magnetism is inhaled through respiration. Could you see it as we do, the greed of the spirits to communicate with mortals on this sphere, you would not then hesitate a moment to develop this gift of yours which will benefit so many in spirit-life and on earth.

Ed, we have a beautiful home; we don't remain in it. As long as there is an S—— in the material form, we will come to assist and develop them. Ed, be patient with your boys, do not debate too much with them. . . . May God bless you, and may you always feel that there is a spiritual guide with you, assisting you in working out this great truth.

COMMUNICATION OF JUDGE ELLIOT.

EL — El — El — El — El — damn it, Judge El — (Elliot? suggested by me) yes, I am somewhat confused. (I suppose this is the first time you have communicated?) Yes, it is. That man, Bo — Bo — I can't call his name. (You mean Buford?) Yes, Buford is as sane a man as you are. He will suffer. Remorseful influences will be his punishment. We don't want him up here. We don't want him sent up here. He had a private interview with me before — (It is damn funny that I could not speak distinctly until you put your hands on this woman's throat). He wanted me to accede to his propositions, but I would not hear to them. They will prove him insane, but that will not relieve him . . . (spoke too fast). I have gotten over my scare. I've gotten over that. I will attend that suit. I have power to influence that. I will help (to form the verdict, I suppose) . . . (too fast).

I have power to act and do now, (have as much influence over others as when I was), in the material body.

I tell you there is as much of me as an Elliot, as there ever was . . . There has got to be a change in the laws.

The Constitution can't reach the case. A man's life is not worth that (the medium snapping her fingers).

Judge Edmonds, whom I have met before, brought me here to communicate. Said I would feel better by doing so. I have met Lincoln, Washington, your father, and hosts of others here . . . Good-by ; I will come again.

N.B. — Judge Elliot was shot down in the streets of Frankfort, Kentucky, a few days before this communication was given.

FIFTH COMMUNICATION OF BEN HAMAN.

May 15, 1879.

GOOD-MORNING brother, with love and aspiration we now meet to give you our thoughts. Please read a few of the closing sentences of my last communication (after I had read he continued). It is essential that every woman who accepts the high and holy position of becoming a mother, should study and acquaint herself with the sacred trust assigned to her. Then mortals would be more receptive to the pure intellectual thoughts, impressions (which is spirit) which are daily attempted to be imparted, but which are repelled, on account of the crude physical organization pro- duced from an undeveloped mind.

Just as an apple-tree brings forth fruit, according to its cultivation, depending solely upon the feminine portion of its elementary condition, so the offspring born in this life partakes entirely from the mother's will, nature, and spirit. Do not wonder, then, at so many undeveloped mortals existing on this sphere ; they are produced from uncultivated minds.

Every action of the mind, thought, and emotion of the mother is transmitted, and causes a vibration of a sympathetic chord or nerve in the fetus. Since mind influences the fetus, it partakes largely from the disposition or passions of the feminine will. The will influenced by anger, passion-craving natures, selfishness, envy, and arrogance, all affect the fetus more or less. Now, how essential it is that a mother should be passive during gestation. How few there are that are physically or mentally organized to take upon themselves the holy responsibility of becoming a mother. It is not considered, and little is comprehended of the sacredness of that mission. There is a holy, spiritual emanation that descends from the aromatic spheres of spiritual productiveness, which is imparted to the infant at the moment of its birth, — it is the divine essence of spiritual life. Now, then, understand that that essence in its unfoldment is exactly like what the mind of the mother has fashioned. The brain of the fetus vibrates in unison with every feeling which stirs the mother's brain, consequently the formation of the psychical and mental organs depends wholly upon the mother. Since so great a responsibility rests solely on the female, she should be educated and instructed in the philosophy of human nature. The attributes of love, sympathy, and charity should be unfolded through the development of her spiritual nature. Then she would be more capable of producing better and purer minds.

Through the cultivation of the female mind, drawing them nearer to spiritual things, obliterating the material, giving her thoughts to purer aspirations, her mental faculties will perceive and unfold themselves more to the pure and elevated conditions of this material life, avoiding frivolity and sensuality, cultivating her spirit, aspiring to a purer and brighter spiritual attainment. Cultivating virtue in every sense is her duty; but this has been sadly neglected by the majority of mothers.

These laws and habits once comprehended, will have a tendency to moralize the human race, and perfect it both in spiritual as well as physical habits. It is the violent, angry passion of the mother that develops the germ of contention within the offspring. It is the craving, longing enmity of the mother that develops the germ of dishonor in her offspring.

Now I have given you an outline of the effect of the mind of the mother upon the developing fetus. The father imparts but very little, mentally nothing, physically the whole. He gives by impregnating the semen, the physical life-germ in its essential positive force to the negative ovum, which unites and forms the whole. Without the positive life-germ, the negative could produce no object; when united, the moment of its blending with the ovum the two combine as one, and there is life of the fetus. In this positive life-germ, there is conveyed to the fetus blood and life of the material of the male. Blood which contains the life contains nothing of the soul, simply of the nature of the material. Consequently the father gives from the material, blood and life; he gives nothing of his spirit or will. Some children partake of the nature of the father in their development; not by impartation through the semen, but simply by the father's external habits making impressions on the mother, is any of the mental characteristics of the father imparted to the fetus or child.

The drunkard will make an impression on the mother. Any violent passion, or any kind of mistreatment of the mother, will make an impression upon her. That impression is conveyed to the fetus; it is not produced by her own will, but by the external influences of the father. The father, then, is also held responsible for every unkind act which he may commit through ignorance at that time. If he does a wrong act which shocks the mother, it is sure to make an impression on the fetus. Therefore, the father, as well as mother, should consider their responsibility in the production and care of offspring as a sacred mission, to be performed in compliance with nature's laws.

Children are flowers transplanted from the gardens of spiritual spheres to those of this material planet. The seed impregnated in good soil, when properly cultivated, will bring forth beautiful flowers, delicious in their fragrance, and resplendent in their beautiful colors. Likewise the little child, depending largely upon the material drawn from the matron, grows and expands, its mental attributes affinitizing with and closely resembling those of its mother.

Having given an outline of correct ideas, as to the development of the fetus, I must state, that any habit which the father or his ancestors may have indulged in promiscuously, is conveyed in the semen to the fetus, in the first stage of its development. That, too, should be a study.

They who have a deficient organization are not fitted to become parents, and should not accept the holy mission, for if they do they bring misery and suffering upon themselves and the helpless beings they are instrumental in bringing into this life.

NOTE.—This is the book the Chicago medium told you you were to make. I want you to understand, prophecy can occur now as well as eighteen hundred years ago. B. H.

May 15, 1879.

CONFUCIUS comes from his sphere above out of sympathy and love, helping his brother in his material life to attain power from fruits that are ripe.

I want to give you a little philosophy, dear brother, since we are on the fair road of progress, I wish to speak upon higher intellectual philosophies.

Have you any idea how time is occupied by us in the spiritual spheres? Each one that passes over, if the intellectual germ of identity is developed sufficiently to comprehend the change, takes his place within the spirit sphere wherever his inclination or will draws him. Consequently you will understand that very few ascend to a very high position, being adapted more to the material. Self being essentially material, they give more to the material, and the spiritual inclination being drawn more to the material, they locate where the reflections interblend with their desires. Many of these, returning to earth, being controlled by influences that stand upon materialistic planes, cannot give you the pure spiritual, intellectual ideas that flow from the fount of wisdom; being themselves but pupils in the great school of nature, they are not able to grasp those ideas and expressions at once, but must await the development of their mental faculties, in realizing the true laws which lie round about them; through the unfoldment of which they can comprehend that there is an inner life beyond this material atmosphere which interblends with the purer essences of Deity, varying in color. Their perceptiveness cannot fully comprehend, and if they do comprehend, they cannot give expression to their thoughts, no more than you can all that you feel within yourself. Incompatibility is assisted through nature's laws. Living in the spiritual atmosphere and attended by superior influences, the spiritual perceptiveness unfolds itself and attains a power or strength by which it is able to throw off expressions. Those expressions are received by yourself in your material body, and greatly assist in the way of progression. In this sphere it is a general thing that mortals are guided entirely by reflections thrown off by spiritual beings, causing impressions to be made upon the mental organs of their material body.

Comprehending this as you do, you will readily know why I do not always attend you. You have more than one home in the spirit spheres. "In my father's house are many mansions," for you and all who seek to progress.

It is only by cultivating the mind that your spirit outgrows the lower murky spheres, and ascends to the glorified realms of spiritual law and harmony. None there are that can attain to this elevated position at their first entrance into spiritual life. Through perseverance, energy, and works of love and kindness, by helping each other, by giving strength to one who is weak and frail, too timid to take a step lest he should fall, raising him up as a father would his loving child, through works of love, through deeds of kindness, the immortalized spirit ascends into the spheres of love and harmony. Good will to all mankind, charity for all.

> Be the faithful friend of every child of earth,
> You cannot say of one, he hath ignoble birth;
> For on the brow of every one, though dark that brow may be,
> We trace the signet seal of God in his humanity.
> And when earth's children seek your aid
> You dare not stay your hand,
> For 'tis within your power to aid,
> You hear the Christ command.
> Like wayward birds storm-staid at night
> They'll in your home find rest,
> So you will take those little ones
> And fold them to your breast.

They are little ones compared to you, who have attained so much knowledge, so much power. You can benefit the soul by laying on your hands. You not only help the body, but the spirit also. You reach out into the vacuum of space with your mind that is pure; we impart magnetic power to you; with your assistance they are benefited from our fountain of magic essence.

"In my father's house are many mansions." Where are they located? Looking through the veil which obscures the real from that which is imperfect, you will observe that light and darkness are very distinct objects. The light imparts happiness and gladness to the soul, electrifying the senses, replenishing the mental power with clear perceptiveness; the darkness developing deeds of undeveloped nature, giving shadowy outlines to shadowy things; they dare not approach, but yet through obscure conditions they work in undeveloped material.

Following the light, you observe in distant spheres circle after circle of spiritual souls basking in the sunlight of happiness, interblending with the great principle of love, holding their communion with the superior forces, that add to and replenish their strength through the baptism of the pure magic aura that descends upon them. This aura is handed down from sphere to sphere until it reaches your material sphere, through the monitors, the mediums that are in receptiveness, and diffusing it in the midst of the great human family.

Prayer ascends. Prayer, when spiritually uttered, reaches circle after circle to whatever circle your adaptions or inclinations may have ascended.

Prayer is the expression of the soul or spirit, which your attending guides convey to the next sphere, from thence to the attending spheres, until it reaches the superior intellectual forces, which transmit the response through approximation back to your individual self. Prayers are assistant thoughts that work out material effects.

We have to stop now, this electrical storm interferes with our conditions.

SIXTH COMMUNICATION OF BEN HAMAN.

May 22, 1879.

BROTHER AND CO-WORKER, I greet you,— It is not generally understood that the physical body should be prepared, as well as the mental organs, to make it receptive, and bring about conditions harmonious for the infant. The interblending powers which lie in nature will assist largely in unfolding the faculties of the mother, if she directs her thoughts upon them. They are nothing more than spiritual influences, which can impart impressions on her mental faculties.

The physical body is exactly what its growth hath developed. Spiritual beings cannot add as much to the physical as to the mental. The physical pertains to what it has received in its maturing development from the very embryo, whatever may have been imparted to it from its progenitors.

Remember, always, that diseases are imparted by the father, as well as by the mother. Consequently, diseased physical bodies should never submit themselves to give life to offspring. In doing so they sin against nature's most holy laws, and the sin not only imparts suffering to themselves, but to generations of sensitive beings compelled to live out a suffering existence. An ignorant man, in the dark envelope that surrounds him, cannot see this, cannot see the error he is committing, in thus giving himself up to passionate desires and sensual lust. It is therefore essential that more attention be paid to this philosophy, the teachings of which, in time, will unfold the faculties of the race, bring them nearer to the pure influences, and make them receptive to impressions imparted to them through magnetic assistance, which gives strength and power to the will, which is spirit, to control those passions, which have been imparted to the individual body or soul by the parent.

When seated in a magic circle of minds that are desirous to be benefited, the animal magnetism so termed will assimilate itself. In this negative state, the positive will-force in the magnetic power comes to the assistance, equalizing temperaments by impregnating the physical body, stimulates the soul propensity, and makes it fully receptive to spiritual influx; adhering to the purer thoughts, which are spiritual emanations, in advice imparted by the soul principle, which gives expressions to the spiritual nature of the individual. In this wise developing the spiritual nature of the individual toward purer thoughts and purer aspirations, imparting a tendency to aspire to higher and more intellectual truths, throwing off the material adherence, aspiring to purer thoughts, purer works and deeds, wholly outgrowing, as it were, the material, which is crude and gross. Where a mind has a tendency to interblend with pure spiritual things, it outgrows the crude material of this life, and interblends with the more ethereal. In this wise you make conditions for the spiritual forces to assist you.

When this position is attained by mortals, they can no longer assimilate themselves or associate with the crude material beings of this sphere. Spiritual intellect develops a diversity of thoughts which, having their origination in the superior spheres, have a tendency, a power, to draw the mind above earthly things. Consequently, by paying strict attention to thought conditions, one cannot avoid developing the better part of his nature; for sincerity and truth make conditions for the superior forces to interblend and assist. The spirit grows in strength according to the intellectual unfoldment or what it may have acquired of knowledge. Consequently, the mode of teaching here does not impart to all alike, and cannot unfold the same comprehensive power in every individual.

*Objective teaching makes a deeper impression on the young mind than that which you compel through reading or by their own mental absorption. Advance (present) an object, and you have assistance through influx, which throws off expressions; and those expressions convey to the young mind — which is always a negative more or less — (power to) receive and comprehend them readily. Read historical facts yourself, and if you convey them to a pupil, with a verbal explanation, you convey the force of your expressive will, and make a permanent impression.

The Pythagorean School, founded on intellectual sciences, did not hand down in print, to the pupils of that later day, the knowledge which the great philosopher had acquired. Being students of nature, as well as material objects, they imparted their knowledge to the student principally by objective teachings. The students received through impressions every principle of information they could glean, and through which the spirit might be impressed or educated. In this wise the spirit acquires the power, the knowledge, and full benefit, which unfolds the intellectual powers of the mind, and gives it the combined negative and positive will-force.

When these forces are more readily understood, it will be easier to teach the pupil through intuition, and confer upon him a more permanent benefit. For impregnation of the spiritual mind can never be thrown off if the physical organs hold out in strength.

Education, so termed, is the only source of future power in spirit, and just so long as the spirit is deficient in knowledge and in experiences of this material life, it cannot enter the celestial spheres, but prefers living on the same plane in the spirit spheres.

Knowledge is power, and its potency acts entirely in will-force, founded upon the highest principles of love and truth, which the spirit can only acquire through perseverance, energy, and faithful researches in nature's divine laws. It matters not how many are born in this life, you will not find a superabundance of these souls in spirit, simply because the earthly experiences are essential to the spiritual development in unfolding its attributes, which it can never obtain without repetitions. How very weak, in the way of perceptiveness, is the spiritual intellect in some mortals! It is not always organic malformation. Usually the experience of the spirits has been too limited in their material researches. You must give such sympathy, and have patience with them. They require assistance; their education cannot benefit them much, especially on this sectarian plane; it is too narrow-minded, and can never make conditions for a full outflow of spiritual thought. Mankind must, step by step, advance toward the celestial shores of happiness. Thoughts must become outgrowths — must be thrown out into space, so that mortals can aspire to more intellectual truths; the proof of which we give you in verification is, that spirit cannot become immortal in one existence. We term the spirit immortal who has acquired this power. Few there are who attain their individuality through spiritual growth, and the acquirement of the potent attributes of spiritual power.

You become through a repetition of this life immortalized, adding and re-adding strength to the perceptiveness of your spiritual faculties, the outgrowth of which reaches far beyond to the interior spheres, where the creative power enumerates itself with the interceptive forces of the divine laws, which, in generality, the sense of man cannot comprehend, being too material in nature; not being developed through the sciences of those magnetic laws, he can accept nothing more than his material senses can reach out for.

Many had rather this physical, material life would continue as it is, as long as their material wants are supplied. Many who are material in their habits would prefer to live on this plane, it being more agreeable to their senses.

What would you do with such, but place them right upon that plane? How many centuries they pass in that state we will not enumerate. However, when the spark as a vapor is thrown over them, some severe calamity or disappointment, behold they reach out — they grope in darkness as it were, they cry forth in anguish and remorse. Some dear one in sympathy coming to their assistance, unfolds his or her love, and lifts them, as it were, out of the darkness into light, placing them on their feet. If sufficiently strong to stand alone they will then comprehend that they must work in a new sphere, in a sphere of self-sustaining power.

When once comprehending this, they soon outgrow their material surroundings and cultivate a power for spiritual work. In this wise mortals are assisted through the various spiritual arts, which interblend in expressions to all alike.

We must stop now, as many friends are seeking to communicate. We are desirous of bringing workers on to the

Christ plane who can accomplish in reform as noble and more lasting works.

The pure outgrowth of the spirit flows in torrents over the human race. Just as the sun diffuses its magnetic strength, adding growth to material vegetation, so our magnetic power must diffuse itself and give strength to perceptive organs to develop and become purer in spirit and more lasting in effect.

We are in earnest, and know whereof we speak. We now can tell you of heavenly things, which the Nazarene could not on account of the ignorance prevailing at that time. Man's nature is unfolding, and yields more to the spiritual influences. Work on, brother, all will be well in the end. I bid you good-day.

May 22, 1879.

CONFUCIUS. — Hope gives you strength to work now, brother, as our thoughts do blend. So love unites us ever in working for a purer cause that draws us ever nearer. I merely wish to say, hold firm. Duty calls in this great work for earnest sincerity and zealous strength. We are banded together. Our souls aspire to truth. We are determined to aid earth's children to aspire in knowledge and truth. Farewell, brother.

COMMUNICATION OF BEN HAMAN.

May 29, 1879.

AS the new light dawns upon man it vitalizes his physical organs. It is nothing more than magnetic force which surrounds every mortal in this life. There are two different kinds of magnetism. The one imparts physical strength, the other mental development. These forces, which lie imbedded in nature's laws, convey the very life principle to the human system of which the generality are ignorant. Not being educated in nature's laws and forces, they cannot comprehend this power and the potency of its benefit to the human race. Education forms character in every sense of the word. For the spirit being drawn out through the mental organ called sensorium, the external verbal power interblends with every thought of the spirit. When administered in a positive way to the negative, which the individual must be in order to be receptive, it unfolds faculty after faculty, and makes the comprehensive mind impressive to the object.

When there is more attention paid to the natural education in the material laws, children will be born with intellectual organizations so that the spirit can acquaint itself with the verbal truths which lie imbedded in nature. This, through magnetic power, is handed down from the superior spheres of the immortals.

Draw the child's mind to an object, though it may not be tangible or visible to the material eye, you can by explanation direct the mind upon a fixed object in spiritual design, and give it the true comprehension, unfolding faculty after faculty. In this manner, the mind is made impressive to spiritual influences, which are the educators of the present age. They inspire mortals with new inventions, which are a benefit to the human race in the way of manual labor, and lighten the burden of toil, giving more rest to the physical organs, making every condition that the human race may pass through experiences of both physical toil and mental advancement.

He who consumes his time in manual labor, the very strain and pressure on the physical body, causes a numbness or drowsiness to cramp his mental powers. Consequently, by lightening this physical burthen by machinery and various instruments, a better opportunity is afforded, and a greater desire imparted to the spirit, to seek after spiritual knowledge. The very faculties becoming more impressive to the material surroundings, it is natural that a desire should develop itself for spiritual elevation. A material body in a constant physical strain cannot develop much intellect in spirit. Those organs being strained to their utmost capacity, are unfit to perceive the beauty of the internal truths, which otherwise would interblend to their unfoldment. Physical labor belongs to the lower element; there are beings that must pass through those experiences. At the same time, it is true that by making conditions in lightening the burden of toil, the spirit becomes more sensitive, awakens in strength, and realizes a natural desire for its advancement. If the laborer has the right conditions in his surroundings, his labor can be lightened through spirit influences. His material body becomes sensitive to this magnetic assistance, which strengthens the organs of the physical body and develops the mental capacities of the spirit. Gradually the tide of human progress will advance through this magnetic power, so that the human family will become spiritualized in nature.

Strict attention should be paid to the magnetic surroundings by making conditions in your own family, it being a duty for every head of a family, father and mother, to make such conditions; no matter how weary from the cares of the day and toils of manual labor, after taking a bath in cold water, let all members of the family sit in a circle, extinguish the light and fix their thoughts upon heavenly objects, and thereby open the door for their spiritual friends to come in rapport with their thoughts, and, understanding their material thoughts and desires, work them out to their benefit, also shower magnetism, which is the elixir of life, over them, relieving them of their fatigue, and giving strength to their nervous systems, thus preparing them in every way for the next day's experience, imparting rest and healthful conditions to their physical bodies.

In this wise prayer is heard and worked upon, to the benefit of those who make conditions. No family should be reared without this law of spiritual affinity, which holds good with all developed and undeveloped. For all having their pure and impure attendants in spirit, according to their nature in material, the power of attraction interblends with whatever the thoughts are directed upon.

Let them begin on ever so low a material plane with a sincere desire, the crudeness of the material nature will be thrown off and the purer take its place. All are marching on the same way of progress. No soul was ever infinitely pure in its first stage of development. Certain experiences are essential to draw out the spiritual germ which cultivates itself, after realizing the external forces, and interblends with the purer.

If it were not for evil, there could be no good. Good is developed evil. The undeveloped power must have its essential experiences, and through its achievements the good unfolds itself. There is no human nature that has not the good and evil germ within it. Through the unfoldment of the good, the spirit realizes the benefit (value) of its true worth. The murderer, after having committed the crime, is borne down, crushed with remorse. No matter how hard his nature may be, the sympathetic germ unfolds itself, which is the essence of the most high and divine. Consequently, in recognizing the right and wrong, it overreaches the evil, and develops the spirit. The right is the light and truth; the wrong is the error and darkness. There cannot be light at once. The sun does not throw his rays all at once; he rises gradually, and gradually disperses the darkness with his light. So with the law of progression; gradually the rays of light invest the material body, and the spirit can see more clearly the right from the wrong.

The laws of nature hold good in effecting this through magnetism, and children from the very moment of their birth should be taught these laws and become observers of them. For through the magnetic power this separation of right and wrong will be unfolded, they will learn to observe more strictly the moral laws pertaining to their own physical bodies, which is the first law and should be understood.

Strict attention should be given to every moral principle which belongs to the body. By complying with more regular habits, see how an infant grows from the time of its birth to its third or fourth year: as long as the mother pays strict attention to its material wants, by complying with regular habits and attending to its necessary requirements in the way of food and sleep, it grows in health and strength. After those years if they are not as strictly watched, and there is less attention given by the mother, their wants and regular habits are not so strictly attended to, they do not grow as rapidly as before.

Strict attention should be paid to their habits. A time for sleep, a time for administering food, a time for study, and a time for play. In this wise (if the germs of disease are not inherited from their progenitors) a body attains more strength and larger development, and mental culture develops with more rapidity. All those forms which are overlooked with indifference by the generality of the human family should be understood as necessary to the spiritual development of the human race.

It is high time that the human race was brought out of this ignorance, and freed from superstitious ideas, which have been handed down from one generation to another. Most mortals are now struggling and striving and dragging out a miserable existence, some of them ever trying and never accomplishing much. Now in this nineteenth century from the Christian era, so called, the spirit world has come in close rapport with the material borders of this, and the intellectual forces are handing down through magnetic descent the verbal truths and proofs of their intercession. The human family must and will be benefited, if they make conditions and pay attention to the impressive powers that are influencing the more intelligent minds of this earth.

Every nation in its most undeveloped state will prove to you from historic facts, that superior minds control the inferior. The inferiors require leaders or advisors — instructors to assist them as monitors in teaching them the truths. Christ, the Nazarene, unfolded truths after truths which were not comprehended in their true sense. Wherever he went, he diffused the light among all, and made impressions on one and all that were thrown within reach of his magnetism. Those impressions did not unfold themselves within all; the spiritual nature being of such an undeveloped order with some, they could not. Consequently such could not be benefited; but there were others, those of a more spiritual nature, who received the impression of this magnetic power and it impregnated them with an inspiration that forever adhered to their character.

* Every medium is a receptor of this magnetic power. It does not lie purified right in your midst; it can only be imparted to you through a monitor from those superior ones located in the far distant spiritual spheres. Remember that all is controlled through circles. The centre of every circle is the receiver, and also the dispenser in assisting the inferior; it is handed down from the central force or sublime circle, which is ethereal and is located beyond the seventh sphere; the approximating power impregnates the centre of the seventh circle in the seventh sphere, from that to the sixth, from the sixth to the fifth, from the fifth to the fourth, from the fourth to the third, from the third to the second, from the second to the first, which is located in the atmosphere of your material sphere and is in direct communication with mortals. Do not pretend to think that that is the only circle, for there are numerous circles located in the distant spheres, having connection with various channels interblending with objects

here. It is just like your rivers branching off into various streams — so these magnetic circles, emanating from the superior creative power, interblend with this earth in various ways and through many channels.

May 29, 1879.

CONFUCIUS, — Noble brother, I am here.

> Love is spirit, spirit is divine, and gives us strength to labor
> Within the fields of mortals here, and demonstrate their Saviour.
> How beautiful is life divine, when the reflections given
> Are comprehended, and define their future birth from heaven.
> Yes, love is light, and light is life, the truth we here array,
> And give to mortal minds the strength to lead them in the way
> Of virtue and of purity. Combined here in its strength,
> It gives the spirit power to work, and mind its normal strength.

Our labor is a labor of love, and such should be the desire of all who work in this great cause. The salvation of the soul means, in its definition, the development and elevation of the spirit toward its original affinity, which is God.

Are you not all children of one great human family? Are you not all children of one great infinite power? drawn hither through one great affinity interblending with that superior potent power?

As light in the firmament, as water to the famished traveller gives invigorating strength to his physical body, so this essence divine gives strength to the starving soul, and buoys it up out of its material crudeness into the spiritual ascension of divine love and harmony.

Oh, reflections of celestial light from angel homes! how indifferent mortals are to them! They convey to the soul that soothing balm, which in their unfoldment develops hope within the spirit. Mortals are poor indeed when devoid of that aspiring power which attracts the pure forces within nature's laws to their material assistance.

Hope! without it there can be no happiness, for the soul is impoverished and stripped of that natural gift which imparts the vital power of life for its future happiness.

Love! oh, essence divine! An impartation from both father and mother God, the germ of piety, the germ of sympathy, interblends with hope, and expands through its assimilation the broader perceptiveness of the spiritual faculties.

Charity! Oh, restless mortal, you cannot see the mote in your own eye! He who has not charity for his brother man has neither hope nor sympathy. Those three graces, interblending with but one thought, which the living life-germs impart to all through impregnation alike ; but which through cruder experiences and developments, cannot unfold themselves in the material body, and reach out to benefit each other.

Charity conveys deep thought and force to the human mind. The world is uncharitable with many. The world is charitable ; but mortals are of the animal productions of the planet, and, in general, the uncharitable ones.

You can condemn none, remembering that the spirit of love, the spirit of truth, the spirit of charity, intercedes for all alike. A kind word to the wavering one, a kind look of sympathy to the hopeless one, an act of charity by assisting and raising up the fallen one, are the true precepts of the God principle.

Oh, man! oh, man! reach out for higher truths. You have groped in darkness long enough ; seek the true light, and enjoy its benefits, by observing the golden rule which Confucius has taught to man in the material, and which the Nazarene imparted to those who could receive, " Do ye unto others, as ye would that others should do unto you." You all desire, every mortal desires, to receive the full benefit of that which is to his or her material benefit ; but the majority of mankind are loathe to give the same which they receive. Oh, look not too much to your own material wants, but you who have sufficient for your own, see that your brother is supplied.

Selfishness, arrogance, and animosity must be crushed out. The spirit of liberalism must interblend and come to the assistance of the spiritual nature of man.

Father God is the father alike of all earth's children great and small, the earth furnishing abundant supply for all alike. The great Cause producing an abundance for the human family, none should suffer; and if charity were sufficiently developed in the spirit of man, he would see his duty toward his brother. No material body, with a heart to feel and comprehend, could see his brother in the flesh famishing by the wayside, without rendering him assistance.

This feeling of charity must develop itself within the spirit of man. You must develop the spirit of charity, which is democratic in its nature, and must be universally expended in giving to each one alike his portion, both materially and intellectually.

By asking for the repetition of a sentence, the communicating intelligence said: "You have broken the magnetic chain of thought. Never interrupt. In speaking, you become positive, and break the conditions, even by saying 'Well' when you have written down a sentence, and are ready for more. I assumed the name of Otto Watto, as you were not at first prepared to believe that such an ancient intelligence could interest himself in mortals as Confucius, which is my true name."

Through Mrs. Shirley, a trance medium, came: "You go in deep into Spiritualism, and that is what brings the lofty. Solomon says, 'Foolish, foolish the action of the ancients. Money lavished on idols. . . . Confucius comes; he lived long time ago." Through Mrs. Rich of Boston: "Confucius is your guide."

COMMUNICATION OF BEN HAMAN.

June 2, 1879.

UNKNOWINGLY man walks amid a crowd of angels, who are anxiously waiting to impart a thought that may be to his and their advantage.

I have so much to say to you that it will take time and conditions to impart it in language comprehensible to yourself and others.

Every mortal on this material plane has angelic guides or influences, usually called guardian angels. They are drawn hither through sympathy and love, for the purpose of benefiting and assisting mortals in passing through the various changes and experiences of this material life. Without their assistance, without their guardian care, mortals would indeed be isolated. They impart strength, giving the magnetic power from the spiritual source, which, interblending with their faculties, usually called impressions, aid them in accomplishing designs and objects for the material benefit of the human race.

There are two classes or kinds of influences usually attracted to mortals. The one being cultivated ethereally, the other materially. The one divinely inspired with spiritual power, the other materially endowed with material power. The one divinely endowed can assist the material one, as well as yourself. The individual being the mentor or medium conveys the assistance or impressions imparted by the superior one to the material one.

The material influence remains with you as a protection amid physical surroundings, against accidents, — calamities of any character or kind to mortals constantly standing in danger, through which many escape not knowing how, — always attended with a fright to the individual, which is the electric positive charge imparted to the body by this influence (see p. 56).

The intellectually endowed influence works for the mental unfoldment, bringing the spirit into such a condition that it can work out objects, machinery of various kinds, designs that may impart profit to others, works of art that benefit the human family, progressive intellectual ideas that unfold the spiritual nature of man, spiritualizing the body, causing it to interblend with the purer moral conditions in the human system. Having the guardian guidance of these two opposite powers, you will readily understand why you can assist the one, at the time you are being assisted yourself. The superior power working on your faculties mentally, gives the more material power conditions to develop his own in spirit. His material pursuits toward your benefit is complied with through a law of spiritual development. He, in his undeveloped state, works out a material mission to your benefit as well as his own. He receives only a portion, as a benefit of what you receive.

If you are crude material, only inclined to the crude material, you cannot be benefited much by the intellectual influence. It depends upon the organization of the individual. If the organization is devoid of sensual passions, not given to excessive use of stimulants, or abuse of sexuality, of an even balanced temperament, the intellectual force can work to your benefit and to the benefit of the undeveloped influence. But where those passions are developed, and the individual gives more attention to material things in adhering to the corrupt surroundings of material conditions, he gives the undeveloped influence all the power, stimulating his passions through yours, never feeling satiated (satisfied) with what you receive, ofttimes waiting in the dead hour of night, goading on to crime, and the gratification of sensual desires. The mortal then is under the complete control of the undeveloped. He has made the conditions, having sown the seed he will reap the harvest. The pure and divine influence must then withdraw, the will of the mortal holding him in abeyance; he cannot approach through the impure magnetism to impart assistance.

The aura of the individual co-blending with that of the undeveloped becomes material, murky, and offensive. And not until he feels through a natural desire the necessity of working out of this condition, can he again be benefited by the pure. The benefit can come only by being brought in contact with purer magnetism on the material plane and through material assistance. The germ of his spiritual nature retains the good as well as the evil. When brought in contact with a mediumistic individual, the mediumistic individual can impart to him psychological conditions, through which the superior influence can reach him again, who, impressing him with remorse, rousing the sympathetic nature within him, he will feel the reproach of this influence, which causes deep regret. Never too late to reform. This regret unfolds the superior nature of the spirit, gives him an insight into all the errors of the past, making them repulsive to his spiritual nature which is divine.

The evil part of the spiritual nature is material. Thus good and evil lie imbedded within the nature of every individual. And it lies within the individual's character which germ to develop. If the organization is so formed that material desires are more sought for, the evil germ will be developed and overbalance the divine or spiritual, literally destroying the conditions for its unfoldment. Many there are who pass away in that sadly undeveloped state, giving the evil germ of their nature all the conditions for its purely material growth. The divine intellectual still remains, but not having had proper conditions (on account of its imperfect organization) to develop itself, it enters spirit life with heavier burdens, consequently it remains inactive. The crude material which it has developed for itself is consumed by the elements; the intellectual force remains to seek another material body, to live another physical life.

If the material body or physical organization is so organized that the purer spiritual perceptions and desires can work through, it will be assisted by the divine influence; having opportunities more in harmony with itself, it is benefited working out material desires, which adds largely to the growth of the spirit in identity and individuality.

This power depends largely upon the matrons of this life. Mothers give the organization, the physical body; God or nature gives the spiritual body. Mortals should comprehend that they are creators. They create material bodies, which are the tenements of the spirit. God creates perfect. He gives the germ of life, which is divine intelligence. Man creates imperfect; the majority adhering too much to sensuality, he consumes the nerve power of his system, destroying with disease the life fluid, which is essential in developing organic life.

It is high time that mortals should make this a study, most of them living disappointed lives. No matter what their surroundings may be, the spirit in its tenement feels its inability, its incapacity to work out its experiences; feels the regret, being unable to act and pursue that course which it was predestined to pursue before its incarnation.

Who, then, is to blame, God or man? Man and woman should learn that they must be one, working out to effect in harmony and love, by observing the causes and material effects, positive and negative, in perfecting the human race, by perfecting the organization of every child they bring into existence. If man and woman would study this law, working to benefit each other, they will become as one, the same as God and nature. Father God the positive force, Mother Nature the negative power. Without Mother Nature, the creative positive could accomplish nothing. The positive electric force interblends with the negative magnetic power, giving the conditions to develop and produce every substance that lives upon this globe, from the mineral to the vegetable, from the vegetable to the animal, from the animal to man, the highest.

You must remember that all must pass through changes, minerals existing many million years before vegetation, vegetation existing millions of years before animals, man existed not so many years after the development of animal life.

The next morning I cut from the *Courier Journal* of June 3, the following : —

A TERRIBLE SITUATION.

The Denver (Col.) *Tribune* tells the following story of the Grand Cañon: Charles May and his brother Robert, in the spring of 1870, offered to pass 60,000 railroad ties down the Arkansas from the mountain source: He says, "Our offer was accepted and we started into the upper entrance of the cañon with a large skiff, provided with six days' rations and 200 feet of rope, with which, by taking a running turn around some firmly planted object, we could lower our boat 100 feet at a time. In this way, at the end of three days, having set adrift many hundreds of ties, we reached the entrance of the Royal George. Here we discovered that an attempt to descend the first waterfall with two in the boat was certain destruction, and to return was impossible. Accordingly I determined to lower my brother down the falls in the boat, a distance of 200 feet, give him the rope, and let him take the chance of the cañon (life seemed more certain in that direction), while I would risk my physical ability to climb the cañon wall, which was about 2,000 feet high.

"About ten o'clock in the morning I shook hands with my brother, lowered him in the boat safely to the foot of the fall, gave him the rope, and saw him no more. Then throwing aside my coat, hat, and boots, and stripping the socks from my feet, I commenced my climbing way, often reaching the height of one or two hundred feet only to be compelled to return to try some other way. At length, about four o'clock in the afternoon, I reached a height upon the smooth cañon wall of about a thousand feet. Here my farther progress was arrested by a shelving ledge of rock that jutted out from the cañon side a foot or more. To advance was without hope, to return certain death. Reaching upward and outward, I grasped the rim of the ledge with one hand and then with the other, my feet slipped from the smooth side of the cañon, and my body hung suspended in the air a thousand feet above the roaring waters of the Arkansas.

"At that moment I looked downward to measure the distance I would have to fall when the strength of my arms gave out. A stinging sensation crept through my hair as my eyes caught the strong root of a cedar-bush that projected over the ledge, a little beyond my reach. My grasp upon the rim of the ledge was fast yielding to the weight of my person. Then I determined to make my last effort to raise my body and throw it sidewise toward the root, so as to bring it within my grasp. At the moment of commencing the effort I saw my mother's face as she leaned over the ledge. Presently she reached down her hand and caught me by the hair. Stranger, my mother died while yet a young woman, when I and my brother were small boys, but I remember her face. I was successful in making the side leap of my arms, when I drew myself upon the ledge and rested for a time. From here upward my climbing was laborious but less dangerous. I reached the top of the cañon just as the sun was sinking down behind the snowy range, and hastened to our camp at the mouth of the cañon, where I found my brother all safe. 'Charley,' said he, 'have you had your head in a flour-sack?' It was then I discovered that my hair was as white as you see it now."

Confucius comes from his sphere above, out of sympathy and love. Man must comprehend that he stands superior and godlike in nature. He can add to, or take from, this development. Add, by giving thoughts to the pure intellectual development, which interblends with Deity, the Great God power; can take from it, by adhering to the material of this undeveloped life. Through this divine principle, which is imparted through intellectually defined beings to mortals here, man's intellectual force is increased, and his spirit is strengthened; being guided by a superior force, it seeks to work upon a higher plane. It unfolds the aspiration of love, which is the sensitive activity of the spiritual nature of man.

Life is short comparatively, and yet so much good can be accomplished if mortals seek to interblend with the good, the pure, and the intellectual. This power so sublime cannot reach all in its effects. Minds that are corrupt in their nature, that adhere to evil, material influences interfere with and retard their progress. The pure in nature will develop the faculties that interblend with the sublimer expressions, making conditions for the spirit of love, the spirit of truth, the spirit of harmony, to impregnate their souls, giving strength to the faculties to penetrate and work out their material experiences to their own benefit, as well as to the benefit of those drawn hither for assistance.

Oh man and woman kind! Oh positive and negative material! See that you aspire to more noble attractions, see to the unfolding of your faculties, throwing off the crude material, and that you interblend with the more ethereal and benefit each other.

When you comprehend this divine spiritual power, so democratic in its nature, so potent in its effects, you will seek to perfect yourselves, by throwing off selfish motives, developing out of arrogance, and giving freely of your love to all alike; as God gives love to every creature, so must man distribute it to his fellow-man; be he undeveloped or cultivated, it matters not, he has the germ of the spiritual life within him; he is not to blame for any deficiency of organization. You who have created him are to blame.

The ignorance of the fathers and the mothers is traceable in organizations to the fourth and fifth generation, and even farther on. The nineteenth Christian century (so termed) receives the light which conveys life, new energies, new desires, within the mortal minds of men. That light and life is the magnetic force which is nature, or the negative power of the God principle. It is indeed new to the present generation; having lain dormant so long, unable to work on the human race, on account of its too material propensities, misconceived ideas, and arrogant selfish education. The intellectual powers of the universe have come to their assistance. Few indeed are they who can receive and comprehend, for their organizations correspond with that of their progenitors. They cannot give birth to those intellectual germs that flow with expressions to their spiritual perceptions, until they are brought within the magnetic circle, as Jesus the Nazarene brought his disciples into a circle; when they were gathered together with their doors and windows closed, he imparted the divine spirit of magnetic power to each and all of them.

This pure magnetic essence cannot be beneficially imparted without the proper conditions. The holy spirit of love, of purity, of virtue, is given by us the same as the Nazarene gave to them who were in rapport with him; so we give alike to all those who seek this truth. They will find in our works the pure development of their inner nature, drawing it out externally toward the magnetic sun, which draws it up out of the material atmosphere into the more ethereal atmosphere, where it interblends with superior intellects, then descends through approximating sympathy to the individuals of this mortal sphere.

Oh man and womankind! learn that you are godlike in your caste. Develop the inner aspirations of your souls' sympathies. Learn to comprehend that you can make yourselves happy; that all lies within yourselves. Outgrow this crude material, no matter if temptations are great; cultivation of will-power will control temptations. Adhere more to the spiritual, for that is life beyond the veil.

Reformers and martyrs have suffered in demonstration of this infinite truth. We have lived in spirit-worlds centuries and centuries. The present has developed conditions for our approach to earth; we come laden with truths, with power, with strength, to assist you in the noble work. You too will reap laurels that will waft your spirit above the material plane. You who are sincere will not see the contention, feel the animosity, or realize the arrogance, that is thrown over you; you will be raised above them, being protected by a superior band in spirit, strengthened by their love, inspired by their will, assisted by their work, — you will interblend with them so much, that you will not or cannot feel the material influences that are hurled against you. As Christ you become spiritual in nature; you work upon a spiritual plane, seeking to benefit one and all. As the great Father in his infinite mercy gives succor to all alike, good and evil, so we in our ethereal spheres come to assist you, invoking you to have charity for all alike.

As the fatherhood of God develops the brotherhood of man, so we interblend with pure motives co-workers for this new birth. Spiritual light is magnetic essence conveyed hither through angel portals; ethereal beings who know no anger, that nurse no malevolence, that aspire to love, truth, and charity. Pure motives, wedded to pure thoughts, give strength to spiritual beings whereby they approach and work upon the faculties of mortal man, drawing him out to immortality.

June 8, 1879.

The germ of life is impregnated in everything. Mineral takes its growth from the external magnetic power. Vegetation is assisted through mineral power, the combination of which varies in substance according to the formation. The animal stands a grade higher. The magnetic essence imparts propensities alike to every object on this material plane. However, the object develops in propensity just what its nature attracts. That imbedded in the soil does not attract as much owing to the insufficiency of the supply. The soil or the mineral production is composed of a variety of particles drawn from the solar system, the sun's rays separating in particles in the form of germs, each one developing according to its quality.

Planets after planets have been formed, and are still forming, from these particles thrown off by the sun's rays. They concentrate within the atmosphere, wafted hither and thither through space until a rotary condition is attained. These germs have life composed of a substance that contains nothing but life.

The elementary conditions, imparting a substance of more electric force positive in nature, impregnating these germs with a replenishing force, develop growth that is positive and negative, the positive impregnating the negative. Father God and Mother Nature. These particles, which develop themselves out of this force into material growth, constitute this earth globe. So all worlds are thrown off, or all planets more properly speaking, in particles from the various matured planets. The sun, which lightens this universe, contains this creative power.

Search as you will, you will find no material object in the form of spirit that contains this power. It lies imbedded beyond the remotest space, so far, indeed, that no spirit of mortal has ever discovered its source. We cannot interblend in identity with that superior force. Through researches we discover the vast universal developments, which interblend with each other.

Planets millions of miles distant are in atmospheric harmony with each other; one imparting to the other certain conditions for its development and to its benefit, yet many times to its disadvantage. Those living germs are in constant commotion with each other. The various atmospheric changes perceptible on this planet are often caused by these particles, which are thrown off in electric magnetic atmospheres.

The very atmosphere around you is a mass of living germs, so infinitely small that the most powerful microscope cannot identify one of them.

Comprehending this philosophy, man, the superior force of the animal kingdom, should learn to observe, that by comprehending these laws he will develop himself more in similarity with the creative power. True, upon a material plane at first. However, assisted by beings who have had large experiences in the spiritual spheres, experiences through which they become identified with a power that enables them to work out more correctly the creative power on this material plane. Assimilating as an identity with the animal of the lower order, he should remember, that the germ or essence of spirit is purer, containing stronger assimilation with Deity.

This germ, when impregnated in a lower animal, has not the organization to develop. Man's formation, in physical body, is more like the ethereal archangels', dwellers upon the spiritual planets. The expressions of the creative power thrown off from those planets are intellectual. They contain the purest germs. They are conveyed hither, in form developing purer beings. God created man in the likeness of himself; now, this theory does not hold, that he created the physical body like himself. It is the spirit germ that develops in love, in purity, and knowledge. These virtues assimilating with purer spiritual expressions or reflections, give the spirit its growth. In like manner the human race becomes godlike in spirit through developing the faculties; the mind, which is spirit, can only develop it by searching through the intellectual vaults of nature. The seraphs from the superior planets have developed in purity this spirit essence, which constitutes the spiritual beings of this planet. They embody an ethereal, an external reflection of the internal perception. Man on this planet resembling in likeness, in nature, an affinity. Hence the idea of God creating in his own likeness — likeness to the pure.

Man must learn that he, too, is a creator, and by observing the laws of spiritual philosophy, he will learn to perfect the human race. He stands in the midst of undeveloped surroundings. Nature in its vegetable growth has not yet attained its full development. The mineral changes of the globe are still in activity and commotion; many thousand years will elapse before this commotion ceases. However, man must learn that through the changes of these laws, the atmospheric conditions become purer. The plagues of the ancients are ceasing. The atmospheric changes of those latter days conveyed the poison germs which destroyed whole nations, some affected nations with antagonisms. Why? they inhaled them through respiration, causing depression (confusion) of the spiritual faculties. Man could not reason then as he does now. The spiritual powers were as potent in those latter days as they are now. They could not reach man's spirit, on account of the crude aura which surrounded him, nor could different ideas have been imparted to man, on account of his crude organization.

You understand thoroughly that every nation has had its reformer, whom it deified. Owing to certain influences, attracted thither through a flexible organization, there was an incarnation of a superior intellect; not from the spiritual spheres surrounding this planet, but sent thither from planets remote, the beings of which are thoroughly matured in their spiritual development, the germ of which seeks to unfold itself for the special development of the human race. These reformers can only impart such knowledge as they are able to unfold through the organization of the material mortals here. These spirits contain very potent sparks of magnetic power, and develop man more and more toward spiritual things, but give conflicting ideas at times, on account of the deficient organization of the body. However, intellectual forces from the spiritual spheres have come to their assistance. This germ develops more readily now. Man is not as barbaric as of old. Spiritual sympathy interblends with his nature, and gives the soul strength through which the spirit attains power.

Millions of years have passed, in the beginning of which man was upon the animal plane, and it is only through the magnetic assistance (coming) from the interior spheres that he has been brought out of his barbarity up to his present state. He must learn that intelligence holds close connection with the seraphs and creative powers of this planet. He must strive to perfect the race by observing conditions necessary to the development of the physical body. When given a perfect organization through harmonious mental conditions, the spirit can perfect itself by experiences on this material plane.

There are spirit creators also, just as man creators. Their work differs somewhat from the material in this — they have acquired power through knowledge, and control through will force; working upon electric matter they perfect themselves more and more. The further they advance in space, the nearer they approach Deity. There is no idleness there, all is activity.

When the spirit leaves this body, which man has given him, through vegetating he has perfected that body — with proper surroundings he has developed the organs, so that the spiritual guides could assist him — and has become strengthened in spirit through experiences and assistance, he enters upon the new life, borne hither with the assistance of those guides, and takes up in spirit a character exactly the same as that he lays off in the material. Desires within the spirit which he left unaccomplished, he will seek to accomplish here. Nor can his views be changed, unless his guides have power to assist him — that, too, depends largely upon his own mental development. He cannot accept more than he can comprehend; and if the spirit has not attained development and growth in the body, it certainly cannot out of the body. Therefore it is necessary for male and female to study the laws of nature, and observing (and obeying) them, give perfect organizations to their offspring.

Harmonious conditions with the mother will develop harmonious conditions in the offspring. Nor should there be an offspring forced upon the matron, for that produces a demoniac nature, which can never assimilate itself with the purer spiritual atoms of inhalation. Like attracts like, from the material on up to the spiritual. The rose that is red in color attracts the magnetic aura which develops it with that brilliant hue. And so we trace it from the vegetable kingdom, in its thousands of varieties, to the animal, in its thousand varieties, to the human in his thousand varieties. Every thing passes through a change. Observe the vegetable closely. You can only perfect it by cultivation ; giving conditions to the mineral in its soil promotes its material development; its flavor develops with its perfect growth. So with the spirit of man, it develops with the vegetation of the body. A gross organization cannot develop a pure spirit. Giving too much to the material, the spirit is drawn to the material — desires only to gratify the material, consequently it adheres entirely to the material.

Through cultivation of the body, by living and observing the laws of nature, which are the laws of God — through nature these laws are made tangible to the sense of man — acquainting yourselves with those laws, you will seek to develop out of this crude material. Education, which is knowledge acquired, gives you strength to penetrate and comprehend those fixed laws. In violating the laws of nature man comes in conflict with the spirit. The spiritual body suffers — the spirit will reproach many times. In his ignorance man imagines that God or Deity reproaches.

The laws of God are fixed, through immutable will. They cannot be changed; for that produced through the electric power must remain forever. The human race is subservient to this power; man can live in harmony with those laws if he seeks to comprehend them. If he violates them he must suffer the consequences. Reason in spirit is sufficiently developed with every material individual who has the five faculties to comprehend that in violating the law, which requires replenishment of the body — in violating the law of diet, by taking too much food of any substance or kind, he will cause suffering to the body. By subjecting himself to a draught when overheated he changes the conditions too radically, which closes the pores of respiration and causes fever. Those laws hold good in every experience that man passes through, and should be instilled into the minds of mortals. God does not punish them, but they punish themselves in violating the laws of nature.

TENTH COMMUNICATION OF BEN HAMAN.

June 23, 1879.

I AM happy to greet you, brother! God bless you! The law of nature in its harmonious action reveals natural facts, which should be made a study by mankind. Harmony interblends with everything. It is the outgrowth and ingrowth of all created objects. It proves the love of God or creative power in its most efficient form. God is a father of love, and diffuses it in the atmosphere in harmony with every object. It instils itself within the nature of man, unfolding itself gradually through his sympathetic nature, giving to his character, through spiritual unfoldment of that divine principle that lies imbedded within, a true resemblance of the divine father, becoming more like in spirit, through love and purity.

To regulate more effectually the human race, it is essential that men and women should be guided by the intuitive laws of nature, observing especially the creative law of life. As before stated, men and women are creators. They should be guided by prudence and sincerity. The purest motives should be directed to this — the production of life. Depending, as it does, upon the individual nature of man and woman, they must learn to understand that regularity and order are heaven's first laws. There is a time for everything. When the law is more thoroughly understood, mortals will realize this; they will regulate the time when sexual intercourse is to be indulged in, for the production of offspring, observing it in nature's laws as well as in their own material bodies.

To produce more perfect offspring, there are three distinct rules to be strictly observed and complied with.

First. The female must be inclined through natural desire to infold with the male — in harmony with everything that may aspire towards material as well as spiritual development.

Second. Man's organism must be in perfect health, so that the vital power, which is drawn from the brain in the form or material of semen (which contains the life-germ for the soul's development), must be healthy and pure, so that its impregnation may constitute a healthy body.

Third. Observing the time when nature is the most positive — in the morning, before, or at the time the sun rises. With the rising of that solar body — the interblending of the magnetism thrown off from the upper spheres and conveyed here, imbues mortals with fresh magnetic force, which gives the system vigor, strength, and new life force.

These three conditions should be first strictly observed. Then when impregnation has taken place, the matron should watch every action of her mind, abstain from dislikes, hold herself aloof from low material associations, interblend with such as may impart pleasure to her, studying the firmament, the stellar system, living in admiration of God's creative powers, in harmony with all around her, making efforts to unfold her mental faculties, and abstaining from everything that may cause her to feel irritable and uncomfortable. Diet should be purely vegetable, no meat, plenty of fruit, no stimulants, milk and water the only drink.

In this way healthy and intelligent offspring will be produced with natural organizations, and the spirit imbedded within for unfoldment will be flexible to spiritual impressions. Through various changes natural to the organization, the spirit incarnated will have power more effectively to work out the design, the mission for which it has entered upon this material life. Love and sympathy, being inherited from the matron, develop externally. By the spiritual development of the faculties, selfishness, arrogance, and ignorance are overcome and disappear. These antagonistic points are born with the nature of man. They are impregnated before birth from both male and female, and grow with the development of the physical body. Impure thoughts, indulged in by the mother, make a deep impression on the fetus, and are sure to develop themselves when born into material life. We cannot impress too deeply this fact, which should be understood by every woman in the land.

Thoughts indulged in before puberty make their way and impress the fetus just the same in power as spiritual thoughts impress themselves on you. Pure thoughts give pure desires to the unborn fetus. Remember, the organization depends on yourselves. So with the spiritual reflections, they make impressions upon you, and if your organization is in such a state of development that it cannot feel the pure influence, it receives the undeveloped. I am sorry to say that more undeveloped organizations are born into material life than perfect ones; the imperfect predominate owing to the ignorance predominating.

Notice one woman married or mated to the man she loves. How much she admires any trait of character which he may possess. With what doting fondness does she follow him in spirit and material! If he in turn is kind, loving, and sympathetic, the angel watchers observe and follow them. Where mutual love and sympathy exist, they know the offspring born from such a union will have a perfect organization for some spirit to work out his earthly experience. The right feeling must exist between both. As the angel said to Joseph, "That which is impregnated in Mary is Holy." It was begotten in love. Consequently the angel charged Joseph to take good care of her, to be kind and loving to her, so that its development in fetal growth might be perfect. Now, I charge you all who contemplate maternity, to think seriously upon the object. It is not merely the enjoyment of sexual indulgence. When sexual passion is gratified, all pleasure is gone, but that which follows is that which should be considered — the human soul which is to be born into life, for which you are both responsible. Being God's creatures yourselves, you produce creatures like unto yourselves. If you permit sexual passion and gratification to be the object of your desires, you produce a crude material organization, the soul of which cannot unfold in pure spiritual aspirations. The organization will be deformed and adhere only to sensual things; the attendant spirit unable to penetrate the mental cerebrum cannot work out intellectual benefits. Such mothers stand upon the animal plane; the spirit cannot comprehend anything above their material standpoint. It cannot even be cultured by education, for that germ is imbued with a grossness which cannot be thrown off, but lives to gratify in its development that craving desire in which the organization was begotten.

God's laws are perfect; follow them that you may produce a perfect child. In one sense, education forms character. When the organization unfolds itself to the more spiritual, the intellect grows in advance of the material. But when, on the other hand, the organization unfolds toward the material, a crude organization is produced which must remain dormant to the external beauties of the inner life.

Children should be cultivated the same as you cultivate plants, with care and tenderness. God never intended that brute force should be used. All is love and harmony in nature, as before stated, and should ever be found in the home.

Children should be instructed from the very moment of conception. Kindness from the father toward the mother unfolds the germ of gratitude within the mother toward the father, which makes an impression on the fetus, unfolds the organs of the brain and makes them receptive to impressions.

Born into material life, it should be loved and cared for with all the sympathy that the two can give. Mothers should also understand, that it is to their future happiness, both in their material life as well as spiritual, *to love the infant before it is born.*

During gestation, care should be taken to give all that is to its benefit and growth towards perfecting the body.

When mothers direct their attention to this, and become real and true mothers to the unborn, in feelings of love and sympathy, the same as to those already born, they will impart to the organization in fetal development the germs of love, sympathy, respect, preference, morality, and force of character, which are the beautiful attributes of the psychical organization.

Then culture with care those little buds, that they may blossom and develop into perfect flowers. You are their material assistants. You make their material conditions so essential for their expansion, unfoldment, and growth to maturity. You give the material substance ; see that you study this law and comprehend it.

Hundreds, yes thousands, are sent back into spirit-life before the bud expands. Strict attention should be given to diet. Milk and vegetables should be given for the growth of this delicate bud, which now born into this material atmosphere, requires a change of diet, and treatment similar to that which the placenta has furnished, cleanliness of the physical body. The fetus having grown in water, living in certain conditions, which water imparted to its growth, requires the same in material ; two or three baths a day, an immersion of ten or fifteen minutes, will give the limbs strength and the body vitality, by which growth develops. The germs of disease, lying in the atmosphere as they do, are not attracted to the body when those sanitary conditions are complied with.

After the bud has expanded, in the seventh year a change occurs. The time for the more positive magnetism to take its effect has arrived. Attention then should be paid to the spirit, cultivating the mind through objective force. The spirit is naturally drawn toward its own pursuits, those in which it seeks to perfect itself through its (material) experiences. Consequently you can only give moral instructions through fixed objects, illustrations, and so forth.

N.B. — Several months after the above was communicated the following, in answer to questions, was given at the "Banner of Light" circle through the organism of Mr. Colville: —

"Too many mothers have their thoughts and feelings sent out to material things; far too many mothers feel that to provide for the physical wants of the child at the time of its birth is all that the child needs; but from the very day of germination the child should be taken care of as kindly, as lovingly, as the rare plant in your green-houses, lest the transplanting from the tropical clime may kill out its nature. . . .

"If fathers and mothers were in a condition to become such, with purity of motive, with love surrounding, they might give birth to an immaculate child. It is only the absence of perfect purity of love between parents which prevents every birth from being an immaculate child.

"The law of parentage is the law of God. The law of God is perfect enough. Your obedience to that law is imperfect. God does not require to change his law in order to produce a perfect child."

COMMUNICATION OF JUDGE EDMONDS.

June 23, 1879.

WELL, I see that you are in earnest about this great and noble work. One who sees the spiritual light, which is truly life, in the right sense, certainly cannot help but take an interest in the diffusion of it. Oh! there is so much good can be done, and so few sincere workers. Friend S——, there would be plenty of good mediums if they were not afraid of society and its effects.

Speaking of Spiritualism, it is one of the most high and pure attributes of God. Men cannot make it popular. It is too pure. It works out its own effects, in identity of which it will develop pure truths. Consequently men must become better who understand and follow out the teachings thereof.

It undermines the sensual nature of man by giving him an insight into the purer philosophies of life ; consequently all who are drawn within its atmosphere must become morally purer and better.

You have a very large band. . . . In the first place you have a pure, earnest, and sincere medium, one who would not hesitate to do good, nor would she deviate from the path of duty, though it might be largely to her material benefit.

I truly deplore very much that mediums are subject to persecution as they are. But with firmness of will and determination they can overcome those obstacles ; for the strongest force is on their side. Let them have patience ; let them persevere in this great cause. Truth will live forever ; error must perish. This power must and will unfold itself with all potency, and will benefit all who investigate with an earnest desire to learn.

Mediums have all on their side. Intellectual spirits are sending their power to them. Re-enforcements always coming, victory is nigh. Error must be cut down. Truth must and shall predominate.

ELEVENTH COMMUNICATION OF BEN HAMAN.

June 30, 1879.

Good-morning, my son! Now we have come together to impart thoughts that may be a benefit to the human family.

EDUCATION has much to do with forming the character of the individual. Consequently it is the duty of every individual to study the laws of nature, to acquaint himself with facts that will appear as tangible objects before him. These facts expound the knowledge, the potency of which will develop the faculties of the human spirit, — develop a more liberal and progressive nature, — and imbue the mind with the high attributes of the Divine creator. You have had too much of this materialism — entirely too much is given to the material nature — too little to the spiritual nature of man.

Parents must learn to realize that it is their duty to pay strict attention to the spiritual development and culture of their offspring. Not in binding them to any creed or dogmatic form, but in instructing them with the knowledge that they are developing their own creed. A creed which unfolds within every individual. Through the development of their faculties they will develop a creed within themselves to correspond *with the perceptive power's harmonious blendings of nature's laws.*

Liberty to man, woman, and child, the love of a united brotherhood and sisterhood, having patience with ignorance, controlling it with love and sympathy. In this wise alone can you draw out the magnetic germ of perceptive life.

Children require love, harmony, and sympathy to rear them with positive force. Unkind acts make an impression upon their undeveloped mental organs. They imbed themselves and incite a revengeful nature, dwarfing the intellectual capacities to that which is good and pure. Holding them in secret fear cultivates treachery and arrogance, instead of the divine negative sympathetic nature of God's highest attributes.

O parents! strive to comprehend that in the rearing of children you have a sacred mission intrusted to you, — a mission the responsibility of which you are held accountable for in years to come. Centuries of unfoldment cannot erase the misconceived (erroneous) ideas impressed by a superficial and false education which you, out of oversight, may have neglected to correct. It is your duty, then, to be matured yourself, that you may be capable of instructing the young minds that are brought hither through your influence. You are instrumental in giving them the physical conditions; you are also in duty bound to give them the spiritual conditions, remembering always that the spirit in its new unfoldment in spiritual realms sees things more clearly, more definitely, than you can in your material body. Consequently you are drawn back to earth to work out that which you omitted through ignorance and false education.

The attributes of love are imbedded within the spirit, and if they are by any means obstructed in their sojourn in the body while in material life they, through natural laws, retrace their steps, wending their way toward the material atmosphere of this planet, striving to make amends for the errors of the past. Man and woman by studying the laws of nature can acquaint themselves with facts, which through intuition develop their spiritual faculties, imparting to them a power through which their spiritual guides or controls can and will assist them.

In educating with objects the minds of the young you can, by explanation and reasoning, unfold the faculties — the minds of those little ones. Keep them in the straight radii of your own effulgence. Remember they are like a piece of putty; you can mould their cast, in form and principle, just as you desire. Let it be the desire of every one to mould them in the likeness of God the creator. The more intellectual the development the more moral the habits, and the more godlike in nature they become. Never strive through compulsion to force any obtrusive idea upon their minds. Allow them perfect freedom to expand, that they may take in that which is to their material and spiritual benefit. Care should be taken that they are not influenced by minds that do not stand upon an equal basis with your own foresightedness.

There should be a time set apart in every well-regulated family for spiritual communications, once every day, in order to make conditions for the heavenly messengers, who are interested in your material experiences, to give you assistance in the rearing of those intrusted to your care. Oh, how much lighter the burden of care would be! How much they can relieve you remains to be tested within every individual's self. Their interest in your material and spiritual welfare is far greater than you can imagine.

Their desire develops out of the purest love, and is ever ready to give such instructions, such information, such assistance, as may be to your children's and your own lasting benefit. Through these heavenly visitors you receive intuitive knowledge; when based upon a moral standard within your own self you will have power to lead others. The golden rule of Confucius will ever be before you, Do ye unto others as ye would that others should do unto you.

Parents should keep this responsibility ever before them, of giving opportunities to their spiritual attractions; by making conditions for them to communicate they will receive the power of the Holy Spirit which will assist them. The heads of every family, which consists of father and mother, should realize this, should also understand that there is a divinely inspired influence that keeps watch over every household. That influence is an affinitized soul drawn hither from the superior spheres of the immortals. They are the deputies of the central power which composes the universal power of the family circle, located in the far distant spheres of seraphs and cherubs. They do not hold verbal communication with earth, but send their thoughts as they do through the emanations of their will, which are conveyed through an approximating power to the children of earth. Every family has its central attraction which consists in the moral force and pure development of this spiritual power.

You look upon an infant as the weakest thing, born in utter helplessness, dependent upon the sympathy and charity of its progenitors. The Creator creating animals of the earth, and the amphibians of the ocean, and fowls of the atmosphere, all in rotation, with their peculiar development, placed each specie or kind in a position where they can assist themselves, walking, swimming, or flying; only the young of the human race are helpless and dependent.

The intellectual care (required by the young) which should be understood or comprehended by individuals, will impart to them the knowledge why the human young alone should be utterly helpless. Simply, this will give you an insight, that, from the very beginning, man is dependent on man.

With careful attention and constant handling you give the little waif magnetism. Your spirit guide imparting the magnetic propensities requisite to its physical vitality. The moment the incarnation takes place there is assigned to it a spiritual guardian who holds constant vigilance, many times using means in controlling such material conditions that might retard its progress in its future experiences. This is in every case a truth, many times upon the undeveloped plane, when the intellectual forces cannot approach; the conditions are then controlled by undeveloped influences. The higher cannot obtain power immediately; but in after years, through psychical and careful instruction, the influences yield to the higher law — the undeveloped withdrawing, giving conditions to the superior.

In this wise man is carefully instructed in the natural

forces of nature's laws, developing faculty after faculty, interblending with the more powerful, unfolding the several attributes within the nature of himself. Looking up as he does, the unfoldment of the spirit grows in strength and in power; and, through constant development. interblends with the superior intellects of the spirit spheres.

Ever remember that there are but two progressions, the one upward, which goes toward the divine infinite, by which the spirit becomes strong, firm, positive, and holds control of the physical body, over-ruling every undeveloped desire, and advances with a constant growth towards purity. Just as the fig-tree throws out new sprigs in its growth, every new petal delicately formed, pure, and transparent-like in color; the lower branches and leaves becoming hardened from atmospheric exposures become firm and strong, and repel the storms which beat against them. Now and then a sprig may be torn off through the positive force, but the young twigs hold their position, holding to the trunk. In this wise the spirit of man grows upward, every faculty reaching with its perceptiveness into space ; the spirit gradually ascends to the topmost pinnacle of morality, pure love, and the highest principles of virtue. This is upward progression. Every new thought, every form of knowledge, is a staple power aiding the spirit's progressive unfoldment of individuality.

The downward progression consists in idleness, indolence, and indifference. No desire to exert the faculties, to comprehend the divine truths which lie within their reach, holding ever to the material, giving all to the gratification of the sensual appetites, interblending with all the sensualities of the physical material; the germ or essence which is divine has no conditions by which it can unfold itself, but lying dormant within the body, it awaits repetition. There are very few of the soul propensities capable of developing. The soul resembling the body in its exterior is consumed like the body in the change called death. The cruder the material the more perishable it is.

'Now, as the soul partakes from this physical body the magnetic substances which constitute it as a body, it is annihilated or perishes with the body; but the germ — the essence divine, is attracted through certain conditions, to certain localities, situated between the first and second spheres, assuming a color according to its condition or development. It is devoid of a body, but having a luminous aspect, appearing as a magnetic light often reflects (shows) itself in your *séances*. It is but a germ, varying in color according to its power. The color identifies the power which that germ may have developed in its sojourn within the material body. Some are a red white, some blue white, some yellow white, green reflections, varying in hue, according to the magnetic power which it retains from its physical life. Nothing more, all being annihilated. If the soul, which is the body of the germ or intellect, is not purified through its experiences while in the body, which is the reservoir upon which it feeds, it cannot separate itself from the body. Unless it becomes an identity separated from the body it must perish with the body. Now understand — the body is the vegetation, the spirit is the cultivator and must therefore control, through will-power, the body, and must strive to adapt itself to the higher intellectual forces, of which I have given you an outline.

All depends upon the spirit's cultivation; through its knowledge of these forces it controls the body, awakens within it more pure desires, encounters and passes through experiences which are to the physical benefit of the body, and, as it were, spiritualizes the body.

This is the destiny of man. He must learn to know, and fully understand, that he is thrown upon his own resources; that upon the education he receives he depends in after years. Education forming the character, the soul and spirit realizing the experiences, work on toward fulfilling the desired experiences. It makes, and works out at the same time, its destiny. Whatever may be the experience which the spirit may desire to attain, it will seek to work it out effectually.

Many times through progressive laws, he deviates from the first impulses, is led up through the inclination of his own will, in and through a superior channel, which affords him opportunities to work out more effectually these material experiences, in the accomplishment of which — in the fulfilment of every design — he adds new laurels to those already won.

Men and women are outgrowths of thought. Thought is a power by which intellect is developed. Intellect is a power by which knowledge is attained. Knowledge is the potent power which gives individuality to the human race. If the cultivation of this jewel is neglected, downward progression is inevitable. Observe the progress of the human race, a reaction is taking place. Humanity is learning that ignorance and bigotry (going hand in hand) have been the greatest enemies of progress.

The human family is striving to raise itself above bigotry, which has no head and cannot think, neither has it any foundation on which to build. It is trembling now before the positive progressive minds on the continent. It is an evil that roots itself within the unborn babe; through erroneous education, it has cloven to man, and with iron shackles holds him chained to ignorance and superstition. The new dispensation, which is the spiritual light, has come to his relief. It will teach mortals with tangibilities, which prove that God or Deity is a father of love and not of wrath, is the father of sympathy and not of revenge, is the father of charity and not of arrogance. The three divine attributes, love, hope, and charity, are emanations from that divine trinity which interblends within the soul of every mortal, and can only be drawn out externally through the natural education, which is the *Liberal Spiritual Philosophy.*

COMMUNICATION OF CONFUCIUS.

HOW few there are who comprehend and apply the right means for their development. Love and truth flow from above and give the spirit strength to comprehend with indefinite conception the great Creator. In mercy there descends the sympathy and truth which flow into the human soul and thus develop the truth, that mortals too will seek to comprehend at last the beauties and usefulness of this material task. There is nothing that this power of love cannot unfold to mind, if mankind will seek to comprehend and study nature so divine.

Dear brother, few there are in life, who when withdrawing from the great multitude can realize the Infinite power of God the great Creator. The attributes of love, of purity, of mercy, are imbedded within every object that the human eye rests upon. Man is so crude in nature that he cannot realize the attributes of this infinite power. And yet as the bud unblown unfolds petal after petal, so the human mind, through its researches in nature's laws, unfolds faculty after faculty, comprehending in its gradual development the Divine truths that unfold themselves within the *vacuo* of spaces. How firm in decisiveness should the spirit of man develop itself! How strong in will! Through experiences these powers imbed themselves. He will learn to comprehend that there is something beyond the mystic veil which gives power to the soul, and that is knowledge, which is a power that imbeds itself within the spirit, which impregnates life. Life which is awake to all perceptiveness. Life which is active to all changes. Life which predominates over all material. Life which controls universally in the superior intellectual spheres. The spirit of man will ride the waves of time and control the powers of the universe. In his first stage of development he is as a grain of sand, inactive, incomprehensive, and dormant. Gradual experiences imbedding the life through electric forces of nature's laws, change after change in succession will in time give strength and vitality to the spiritual unfoldment.

Oh! think of it, ye children of men, think of yourselves created as you are in purpose what ye make yourselves. Think of what you can attain, of what you can produce.

The first minor experiences are but as those of a butterfly, living for a time to vegetate in material strength, then perishing, as it were, in spirit with the material. The intellectual germ which interblends with the great infinite, receiving through attraction a little life in addition, unfolding as it were, gradually the perceptiveness of a purer intellect. In passing from one stage to the other, man ascends in knowledge toward the infinite mind, which sustains and gives life and power to all who strive upward and onward toward the realms in the distant spheres of love and harmony.

Seek and ye will find, oh, man! seek that knowledge imbedded within the laws of the universe. Bind sheaf after sheaf, applying it with the purest motives that the soul can comprehend. Knock on the door of wisdom, and it shall be opened unto you, and reveal gem after gem of the beautiful truths which lie within reach of all progressive minds. The father of love imparting conditions to every individual alike, if they can through their perceptiveness comprehend, and through their will apply it.

Life is a power which moves the universe. Life is a strength which holds in control the laws of nature. Life is an unfoldment towards Deity, for that potent power consists in universal life.

We will greet you again, dear brother, whenever opportunities present themselves. We come only in compliance with conditions which are in rapport with yourself and medium. Many blessings, and hope that your healths will be preserved for this work which must moralize humanity.

COMMUNICATION OF BEN HAMAN.

July 7, 1879.

GOD bless you, as well as the medium! The morning light greets us with its calm, magnetic rays, imparting conditions which enable us to impart information for the benefit of mortals. We will begin a new chapter; we will speak of

THE TRUE RELIGION.

Reformers of old were workers in the same sphere in which we are now working. They being in the material body, not having the full development of their spiritual faculties, owing many times to a defective physical organization, they could not work out effects as perfect as we now can.

We are giving you views which we observe from a high spiritual standpoint. They gave their views from their material standpoint, having, however, the assistance of controls, who imparted their knowledge and information as perfectly as they could with their material conditions and surroundings.

The human family in that remote age had not progressed up to its present standard. Repeated incarnations make the perceptive powers more and more perfect, give a clearer insight into the spiritual philosophy, which, when thoroughly comprehended, imparts knowledge to all who can perceive it.

This law held good in that latter day. Antiquity imparted much strength to the present development, by which the growth of Spiritualism with its philosophy is sustained.

However, those reformers had not the conditions on the material plane that we now possess. Consequently, the growth of this dispensation will and must unfold itself with greater rapidity, as human minds develop and progress, unshackled from the dogmatic creeds.

The doctrine of the immaculate conception entered the minds of a few mediumistic individuals, who could not comprehend or define it correctly.

Speaking of spiritual conditions in the way of conception, we must reveal to you, that Chrisna, the great philosopher and reformer, who existed three thousand years before Christ, was born under the same star, with the same presentations of spiritual manifestations, living upon the same plane of moral culture; his teachings excited much thought, and were highly appreciated.

The Christ child, born of humble parentage on the mother's side, who was pure and in assent when she conceived. Being very mediumistic in nature, the spiritual influences that attended her could impress her with thoughts that had the power to develop the fetal organization of the child.

Pure and spiritually inclined, she imparted unknowingly the very conditions to the child that the spiritual band wished for their future use.

Being attended by Elisha, Moses, Socrates, Pythagoras, and a host of others, they worked out those conditions, which enabled them to impart their own spiritual nature to the Christ child, — it being ordained and controlled in the section interblending with the seventh sphere, where the seraphs and cherubims hold counsel, and are constantly striving to send their counsel and assistance to the children of this sphere.

The father, who was as material as any other mortal with ordinarily developed faculties, was high priest of the Sanitorium Shanegum, in which the Jewish maiden Mary was a novice, and was drawn to her in love, in sympathy, and in spiritual conjugality. They were affinitized in spirit, and that which took place through the love he bore her, was begotten in the holiest embrace of a spiritual union, and was sanctioned and controlled by the holiest and purest spiritual influences; was ordained by an infinite and superior power, who holds in subservience the universal laws of nature, the multitude of mortal, and the billions of immortal, souls.

When conditions are controlled through and with such a spiritual interest, you can very well depend upon it that some good effects will develop out of it.

The spirit of the Christ child was an incarnation of David the king,[1] who returned to fill out the mission which the world had applied to him, David, the man of God. Having committed many errors in that life, wrongs and evil to his fellow-man, he returned at once. After viewing the results which would take place, he came as a reformer and a martyr.

The present generation, claiming to be his followers, cannot see clearly the true motives, nor can they comprehend the spiritual nature of the Nazarene. Partaking in nature; as he did, from both of his material parents, who were both pure and undefiled and spiritualized in their conjugal love — they imparted the harmonious blendings of their own natures to the child, who developed in his unfoldment the attributes of love, harmony, and sympathy. He was a brother to all. He was a lover of all, his soul flowing out in that immortal love which he inherited from the all-infinite principle. He gave unto all sympathy. His heart unfolded charity for all mankind and womankind.

The human family, at that latter day, were yet too undeveloped in their nature to comprehend and appreciate him in the true light. He advocated the truth of this present spiritual philosophy. He strove hard to unite minds, through whom he would be able to concentrate magnetic force, by which he expected to work out developed effects. He collected to himself a band of twelve disciples, of whom he was the centre. They varying in mediumistic magnetic qualities, he drew them around him, so that he might be enabled

---

[1] See "Strange Visitors," p. 24. "In like manner Jesus, the celebrated child of Bethlehem, had lived a pre-existent life on earth. He had reigned over a people in his previous life."

to test their power. They at the time being ignorant, did not know or comprehend the laws through which he performed those acts termed miracles.

His psychological power predominating over their inferior faculties, he drew them in subservience to his will, and taught them through this magnetic law the sciences of nature. They were not like him in their development, nor could their material organs unfold as readily to the spiritual laws, of which they were so ignorant. Yet gradually one by one, according to his organization, received the psychological effects of his pure magnetic power, and unfolded the attributes of their spiritual gifts according to the perceptiveness of their own individuality. Each one varying in their views — each one demonstrating their individual impressions according to the receptiveness of their faculties. There was not one of the whole twelve who could take correct views, or comprehend that which the Nazarene himself demonstrated.

While he lived on earth, he was the central star. The twelve in mighty circle stood, their number, it was plenty, and like a solar star, stood Jesus in the centre. The power and assistance which Jesus gave to his disciples while he remained with them, gave them implicit confidence in him. He knew full well that through his psychological influence he would be able to develop them into his spiritual sphere. He gave them magnetic strength in all their secluded gatherings (*séances*). He instructed them in the science of spiritual law, as developed and demonstrated in the moral attributes of his own nature, which was godlike and spiritual.

He was assisted by the same band, through his whole physical life. The same spiritual influences that attended him at his birth attended him through all his material experiences. Joseph, being selected by them as a material guardian, both to the mother and child, was a medium. Through him the spiritual controls of Jesus worked out material effects. The mother's mind was kept passive and undisturbed by material cares, was made more sensitive to spiritual influence, and endowed with spiritual magnetic power, which she imparted with strength to the infant suckling. All was controlled in complete harmony during gestation, as well as during nursing.

Joseph was instructed by the angel, or spirit guide, to watch and care for her, in a holy and pure spiritual way; which instructions he did not disobey, but followed with due deference to the holy spiritual monition and the high priest's instructions.

His education was brought about through the guidance of those same influences. They carried him into Assyria. Pythagoras, controlling conditions, brought him under the influence of the Pythagorean school of instruction, where he was united to the Assyrian sects, and lived twenty years in their midst. Having attained the highest development in moral perceptiveness, having developed the magnetic power which lay within his own nature, and which was assisted by the united band of thirteen in spirit, having unfolded the psychological influence of which he now made use with the most astounding effects, he was told by his spiritual attendants to go forth and diffuse this knowledge, and spread the light of the spiritual dispensation, to instruct the ignorant, to develop the wiser ones, and to crush out ignorance and error, and the false teachings of the Hebrew Rabbi.

He girded on his armor, and went forth with implicit faith and confidence in the Divine father and instigator of his spiritual mission, knowing perfectly well who he was in the ante-natal life, and his motives in returning back to earth; and fully realizing and comprehending through his spiritual development his purposes and his desires.

The determination of his will yielded him success wherever he went. The psychological power which he emitted from his pure inner self conveyed to the minds of every one who came within his magnetic circle, a calm resignation and subservience to his will. In this he was perfect. He drew vast multitudes wherever he stopped to concentrate his will. Multitudes were compelled to flock to him, and when drawn within the atmosphere of his magnetism, he imparted to them the psychological principle and God power in nature.

This magnetic power gave their spiritual perceptions strength and comfort through which they felt, no matter on how low a plane they stood, the calm, spiritual harmony and blending of his power. He instructed them and gave them moral ideas, with pure love and with charitable purposes. He taught that which emanated from the fountain of wisdom, that God is the father of love, that in nature he resembled him, that in spirit he was like him, and made every effort toward imparting the same attributes to the whole human race.

The Pythagorean philosophy of which the Assyrians were advocates at that remote day, advocated the most perfect moral laws and principles, and highest purity.

Psychological power, when conveyed and imparted to individuals from a pure mind, must develop pure effects, when continuation and attention are given. That psychological power which Jesus taught, is the very power which your mediums of the present day are teaching and imparting. Consequently we have told you that it is necessary and highly essential that the organs of the medium, through which it is conveyed, should be pure. Immoral teachers at heart can produce no pure effects.

If Christ had been impure in nature, the seeds he sowed could not have sprung up and become deep rooted in the soil of this mundane sphere. He was premature, and could not be comprehended. The psychological power which he imparted was drawn from the spiritual fountain of the God principle.

Controlled through the band of thirteen, who attended him in spirit, he likewise assimilated the same on earth; he making the thirteenth, the whole being conducted and controlled in similarity with the spiritual band of which Pythagoras was the head in spirit. He did not deviate one iota from the instructions and advices which he received clairaudiently and intuitively, but followed out every instruction with the greatest trust and simplicity. He was successful in many instances.

In this trust to your spirit-guides and controls, faith alone holds good. Not faith in God and the salvation of the soul, as your orthodox sectarian creeds define and require, but faith in those spiritual immortals who instruct you in the moral path of duty, to work out spiritual effects by pure and noble deeds.

The impression which Christ made upon those who heard him developed within some the moral bent of their natures; they could not receive impressions in the same light he intended, they could only see and comprehend according to their own material organization. Consequently they misrepresented his views and ideas, which the various sects have taken up, who all claim to be following the great reformer; most assuredly in purpose they desire to be followers, but in design they vary, and cannot comprehend the true motives of his life and teachings.

He now fulfils that which he forecasted. The son of man will come again, though not in the body, but in likeness, resembling the present dispensation. "He will come in the clouds," which is the atmosphere which surrounds your planet.

Eighteen centuries have passed away and more. His development in spirit has attained to such a height, that his influence reflects upon all around you. Verily he is in the midst of you all, not in person as an individual, but in spirit, as a power, sustained by an infinite host of immortals who are contributing their magnetic power in harmony and assistance.

THIRTEENTH COMMUNICATION OF BEN HAMAN.
July 14, 1879.
The influence of Christ's magnetism upon the children of earth.

GOOD-MORNING, brother! we are now prepared to proceed with our work.

The influence of Christ's magnetism upon the children of earth is now perceptible, and can reveal itself to any mind that desires to progress.

This new dispensation, so termed in the nineteenth century, is very old indeed, as old as the hills of Judea. The spiritual philosophy which is interesting so many minds in Europe and America, is nothing more than the magnetic psychological influence of nature's laws, through which mortals, by thorough investigation, will learn facts which will demonstrate to them the potency of spirit-power. Very little has been revealed up to the present time. Its investigators will expound living truths through the development of this power.

As before stated, minds cannot perceive or receive more than their faculties can comprehend, and they will apply it in accordance with their perceptiveness. Consequently you have conflicting ideas given you through mediums. The spirit makes its impressions upon the material organs or brain of the individual; they are moulded according to the perceptiveness of the individual's faculties, any spirit attempting to control those organs feels their deficiency, their imperfections, at once, and cannot force them into flexibility on account of their positive development.

However, the individual himself or herself, by earnest investigation and positive acquired knowledge, can unfold those organs through development.

Development consists of knowledge acquired through will-power. This will-power, through positive determination, will unfold these material organs, and make them more flexible, more sensitive, to the controlling influences or spirit guides.

Therefore it is highly essential that mortals should give their attention to spiritual things, and not harden their organs in pure material experiences, but give to the spirit opportunities which will impart happier effects to the soul.

Jesus of Nazareth entering upon a new sphere when he left earth, his spirit was freed from material encumbrances. Having crowned himself with knowledge through his educational experiences with the material laws of Nature, having acquired the individuality for which he sought, having obtained a superior condition in the estimation of a few minds upon this material planet, after complying with every law requisite for the unfoldment of this magnetic strength, of which he was thoroughly informed, and through which he accomplished wonderful works, he ascended to do his duty.

However, his followers could not make the same impression, nor do the works which he did, owing to their weakness; in many instances, they could not realize the divine impartation of the God-power in magnetism.

After the ascension of Christ into spirit life, he quickly observed their weakness. The promises which he had made to his disciples he quickly fulfilled; but not until after he had revealed to them to make proper conditions, by excluding themselves in an apartment, closing the doors and windows, and they had seen him in a materialized spirit form.

Very little is understood by the impartation of the holy spirit. Each one of the disciples, having developed his mediumistic propensities, was then in a condition to receive a full development, by the assistance of a spirit, in the form of a control. Each disciple was assisted by his separate control during his sojourn with the Nazarene, but was never sufficiently firm in faith; the twelve never having attained their development as individualized spirits, they looked to Jesus as a leader, and depended upon him for advice and assistance; they were many times overcome by weakness and despair. The controlling influences attending them could not in such weak organizations unfold the positive power of their wills.

Consequently they required the positive spiritual magnetism of Christ in spirit, to unfold and give them their potent permanent spiritual power.

This was imparted through Christ and his spiritual band, who now could give more assistance to the disciples. The magnetic conditions having been changed upon his entering the higher sphere; having developed more power within the same faculties, he gave strength to all alike, with the assistance of the united band which attended him while on earth; being more vitalized in strength they gave to the disciples the spiritual power, to work out the same effects, which Christ himself produced. On receiving the Holy Spirit, the disciples spake in different tongues, in foreign languages which they knew not of. (Every individualized spirit possesses that power.)

They could not comprehend nor realize this spiritual power at first, nor could they understand each other, for all seemed confusion. However, through patient observation, with Jesus in the centre who explained all facts necessary for them to know of this great reformation, they did so. He gave them the assurance of his presence; if they would but call upon him, their thoughts would reach him by uniting themselves more closely to him, and keeping in constant rapport with his influence (which in magnetism is conveyed to the object worked upon), power would be imparted to them.

The disciples, having received the assurance of this power, separated according to instructions, each one having attained his development through the individualization of his faculties, coming now into close rapport with their spiritual guides, following every advice, heeding impressions, instructions which led them into the field of duty, where each one worked out the mission imposed upon him.

Through the spiritual influence of Christ they spoke, at times, in their own dialect, and again in that of others more foreign, changing whenever it was necessary, so that their teachings might be comprehended by all their hearers. However, they could not explain, or give expression to any impression or thought other than that which their faculties could comprehend.

In explaining facts they spoke in parables, illustrating their subject according to their educational perceptiveness, and in a manner to correspond with the ideas and comprehension of their hearers.

In that latter day the human family was not educated up to the present standard. Accordingly the disciples, reformers we will call them now, used words the definition of which did not always convey to their hearers the meaning which the reformers attempted to convey. Three or four centuries later, the prelates who wrote, or tried to write, the history and experiences of Christ and his disciples, were not as spiritual in nature as the true Reformers were. They did not study and observe the laws with the acuteness which the disciples had used. However, they comprehended facts, writing as they received and comprehended them. They did not intend to give the conflicting ideas which the reformers of a later day conceived, and out of which so many varying sects have developed.

The sects of the present time are all branches of the great reformer, varying as they do, some weak and some strong. Just as the stout oak which stands firm and erect, heedless of storm and pelting influences; branch after branch may be torn asunder, yet the young sprouts put forth with more vigor and strength, receiving more of the substance from the interior strength. So with the varying sects; they in faith hold to the reformer; some of them not having sufficient faith become extirpated. Those who investigate with more sincerity, straining their faculties to comprehend more correctly, will, in the evolution of time, develop in firmness and strength that power which the great Reformer is imparting to all who seek to comprehend. He stands, as it were, in the centre of this great spiritual revolution. Never in the remotest antiquity do we trace such a revolution, such a spiritual change as is taking place at the present time.

Christ's mediumistic power consisted of twelve definite forms, — phases which I need not explain, as they are already known to almost all Christians. His prophetic words are now being fulfilled : The Son of man will come again in the clouds, and with more power. This is the fulfilment of those words, Verily he is in the midst of us all. The concentrated power consisting in magnetism conveys his influence wherever two or three are gathered together.

This magnetic power is the baptism which he gave to his disciples, called the Holy Spirit. Legions of angels or spirits, one and the same, are constantly going back and forth from this earth, to work out the fulfilment of his prophetic words. Not only in Europe and America, but in the remotest parts of the earth, where you would little think there was any spiritual culture, but where in fact there is greater impression made upon cultivated individuals than here in the midst of Christian civilization.

Christ the reformer, since his entrance into spirit-life, nearing the nineteenth century, has worked more faithfully, and with more efficiency by far, than the preceding reformers, and why ? Simply this : the old philosophers and reformers having acquired superior knowledge and strength, united with the Pythagorean band, of which Jesus the Nazarene is the centre. He being the later-day martyr, having been informed after his maturity of his sufferings and death, was fully resigned, for the sake of the interest and benefit it would eventually be to the human race in salvation, as the Christians term it, of the soul or spirit, but which in reality is not correctly understood. Salvation not consisting in the simple faith in Christ without works ; but in faith with works. Faith in realizing that through his magnetic influence each mortal can be assisted in working out good deeds and noble designs.

He was a martyr. He resigned himself to every fate, suffered pain and deprivation for the sake of truth. Prayed to get in more thorough rapport with his guides and controlling influences ; fasted forty days in the wilderness to set an example by purifying his body for spiritual communion : he gained strength in spirit by abstaining from material pleasures, the outgrowth of which has become firmer and stronger up to the present day.

He died for the truth. His teachings were not understood save by the few, and those few could not convey them in an indelible form to the inhabitants of earth ; consequently the misconceived ideas which have been drawn from the Pagan schools. Throwing out portions here and there, they have as a body an indefinite conception of the great definable truth which Christ the reformer demonstrated.

However, it has not lain dormant ; it has grown in spirit. The great philosophers, the remotest reformers, having concentrated their forces, are drawn towards the centre, where Christ the reformer stands. They see clearly that they cannot make the right truthful impression upon the various sects and races. They interpose their power, and now harmonize with the latest reformer.

However, it will still take time to develop this truth. The trunk of the tree is strong, the roots are deep within the soil, the branches throw out their tubers into the different continents of this earth, the leaves diffuse their aroma, and impregnate the atmosphere everywhere.

Gradually they will exhilarate the sense of man. Through respiration a natural desire will unfold itself, to ascend to the pure realms of truth, the teachings of which will unfold the moral nature of the human race.

Christ the reformer is the tree of life. Look at the millions who are imploring him daily! See the millions of mortals invoking Allah, Omah, Jehovah, and a host of other gods! They, too, were reformers in their day. They strove to lead minds on a higher pinnacle, but were unsuccessful.

Buddha accomplished greater works, but, owing to the ignorance and arrogance of other sects and nations, his power was interfered with, and greatly impaired. However, the more liberal spiritual philosophy still exists in the Bramin faith. Those persons who are individualized powers standing where Christ stood, working to establish the same purposes in effect, have added additional branches to the trunk. They have concentrated their power, and united themselves in harmony with Christ the Reformer. Through the development of their progressive natures, they now work upon the same plane, for the same accomplishment in power and individuality.

Bands of spiritual beings are sent out from this great head or central circle, which is located in the seventh sphere, where their council is daily held. Thoughts and expressions, influences of love and truth, are thrown off, sent hither and thither through space, to the various inhabitants of earth. The more impressive mortals are sensitive to this influence. They through respiration inhale it; they are then called mediums or instruments through whom this power is conveyed to others, and attract more attention from the spiritual universe.

The great Reformer, attended by the ante-natal reflections and the reformers of remoter days, sends messenger after messenger from sphere to sphere, until the influences reach your earth. This great reformatory principle will develop the true spiritual nature of man, and impart the identical conditions necessary for his development, drawing him nearer toward the Infinite Creator whom they resemble in spirit.

It is through this power, when rightly applied, that the

inner principle of man will unfold the sixth sense, which is dormant in the greater number of the human race. The unfoldment or development of the sixth sense, which is purely spiritual, and interblends with the higher attributes of nature, gives strength and individuality to the conceptions of the spirit, and causes it to grow more potent in purity. Consequently, through this unfoldment, the true philosophy of spiritual life will be comprehended.

Some mortals have intellect, and recognize the material qualities of nature. Comprehending as they do external laws of all characters and kinds, their intellectual views or opinions are formed from the evidence they receive through the five senses, and attribute ALL purely to material substances, which are perishable in effects.

If such would but yield to the impulses of their inner natures, they could very soon detect the inner substance which contains the life-germ, and which is supported and sustained by the interior laws, of which they have no knowledge. By turning their thoughts in that direction they would be assisted towards developing the sixth sense, spiritual perceptiveness.

Gradually all will yield. Through a repetition of the spirit it will eventually receive an organization, by means of which it will be enabled to unfold these attributes of spiritual identity, and through natural experiences, essential to every individual, man will in his development acquire knowledge of these facts, and live out a more perfect life in working out good effects, and assisting others in the unfoldment of their spiritual natures. When that time arrives a more rapid progress will take place; for mortals will comprehend more thoroughly the true religion of Christ, and will strive to live out the true principles and moral laws which Christ the reformer taught on earth, and which at the present time are imparted with treble force to the inhabitants of earth.

His teachings, which unfold themselves in the midst of

mortals daily, consist of moral truths, of which mankind have heretofore heard, and yet in many instances are ignorant of and indifferent to. The influence of this magnetic power which is conveyed hither, must first impregnate the individual, and impart to him of the Holy Spirit. Baptized with this magnetism, which we call impregnated, and which you receive in the presence of every pure medium, through whom it is conveyed, you gain strength and courage; though at first very faint, by repetition it unfolds itself and gives courage to the individual to work out its spiritual effects.

Children of earth must seek for this knowledge, they must make an effort to attain it, they must strive to acquire it; and if they knock on the door of knowledge they will certainly be heard, and the assistance will come to them. But they who sit patiently waiting, without exerting their faculties, or exerting themselves to attain a knowledge of these facts, must continue in their blind ignorance. Use the reasoning power which the Creator has imparted to you, develop its strength, and through the assistance of the Nazarene you will receive the individuality and self-sustenance of your own immortal self.

Every branch which reaches out conveys magnetic assistance to the different nations of the earth. Which nations in time will develop out of their errors into the spiritual light of this dispensation. The same love, the same sympathy, the same harmony, interblends with their surroundings as with yours.

The host of reformers that labored so spiritually on earth have concentrated their magnetic forces in rapport with Christ; and now with this new dispensation of power, the Fatherhood of God and the brotherhood of man interblends with every soul, that it may receive the baptism of the Holy Spirit.

This sympathy, love, and harmony are imparted to all

alike through magnetism, and is universally distributed to the children of men. That love, harmony, and sympathy which individualized the character of Christ and illuminated his character, are doubly unfolded within the higher attributes of the individualized power of the great God-principle.

This is the true religion. Time will develop and unfold the purer gems of its teachings. Mortals must develop out of materialism. Orthodox creeds must throw off their shackles; they must become more charitable and develop out of their crude materialism, which can never interblend with the universal love and harmony of God and his infinite laws.

Those branches which are weak must be broken off, and the true power, which emits itself daily from the original fountain of life, will flow out with living truths, establishing a more potent foundation through which all, all are glorified. Purer motives will wed themselves to purer thoughts; and, with obedient will, they will develop the interior power and teachings of the great Reformer. And ever let it be impressed that, where two or three are gathered together with thoughts directed to the spirit band which he controls, he will be in their midst.

And this is the salvation of the soul through faith in Jesus Christ. Faith in his works, of which you ought to be the followers. Faith in his example, of which you ought to be the workers. Faith in his assistance, through the conditions by which his reflections will reach you, not ordained solely on his own plane, but duly arranged and assisted through the instigation of his will, which is the same in effect as the material father's in arranging to influence and assist his son toward accomplishing material success, but multiplied in number by assistant reformers; they imparting magnetic conditions to each one alike, in the spiritual circles which may control.

This is the second coming in spirit, in thought, in will, the works of which will reveal themselves to all who can comprehend the love and truth in which he lived, in which he died, and in which many other reformers have lived and died who have increased and now reveal themselves with more spiritual effects than in former days, and will finally draw forth the finer attributes of the undeveloped spirit and revolutionize, by the impartation of purer desires and more moral principles, the human race.

We may be able to speak of this subject at some future time. We are workers for this great central power. Christ, the Reformer's magnetism, is imparted to us constantly. We convey it through the medium's organs to those who come in contact with her. They receive it according to their own nature. If pure, it imparts pure desires. If impure, it can make but a vague impression which does not last a fortnight. Therefore, mortals must strive to purify themselves in order to hold communion with their sainted ones. They can only attract the assistance of those of a sphere who stand upon an equal plane with themselves. Progression changes conditions and gives them the power to commune with the purer, who give them assistance and sympathy, the theory of which is founded on tangible facts. B. H.

On my return from a materializing *séance*, so-claimed, I had a *séance* with Mrs. Cawein. Without the least allusion to any impression I had there received, Mrs. C. spoke as follows — she being in deep trance :

COMMUNICATION OF ARIOSTA BEY.

September 23, 1879.

MORTALS are so material that they do not look at the bright spiritual side of things, but give all to the present material. Many of them do not hesitate to commit acts and deeds which are wrong, and that obscure and darken the spirit, and hold it chained to earth. So we find things at . . . We see things largely misrepresented there. However, they do some good in giving those manifestations, which are not what they purport to be.

True, the medium is controlled, and assumes the characters that are reputed as manifesting. She is a trance medium, something like this phase (Mrs. Cawein's) in whom the spirit controls the intellectual organs for spiritual purity and advancement. But there, the object is purely material. Instead of the intellectual, it is all thrown on the material physical organs of the medium, she assuming every character. In personating many times her features take on the natural expression of the spirit. Do you not observe the same through this medium at times? We want honesty and sincerity to spiritualize the human family. Those manifestations may make a good impression on some, but on many they produce a doubtful, sceptical feeling, and do more harm than good. It is not well to advise sincere philosophers to visit and witness these manifestations. The deceptive influences are sure to make an impression on them the same as they did upon yourself. I admit she is not always under control, at other times complete deception. Those who visit there must take their chances. There is no sincerity there. It is all a money-making affair. . . .

Your enthusiasm for the material manifestations has been modified. Ben Haman will speak of why you were permitted to go there. He works on a higher plane.

COMMUNICATION OF BEN HAMAN.

September 23, 1879.

GOOD-MORNING, my son! You have passed through experiences; the purpose was good. One year ago, had you visited that abode, you would have been satisfied, and accepted everything as germane and beneficial. Probably it would have benefited you. You were not then on the plane upon which you now stand spiritually. All must pass through changes. There are many on that plane who are truly benefited by witnessing those manifestations, though it will be very humiliating to the sensitive when he discovers that misrepresentation has been practised upon him. Nor is it right or just to misrepresent spiritual influences or manifestations. However, it is all controlled under spirit-influence, and presented on a plane, which is almost purely material.

We permitted you to visit there, to show you the diversity of power in manifestations, the diversity of thoughts, and their effects upon mortals in this life.

All this does very well for materially inclined individuals, and is essential, for it is a portion of what human mortals are composed of. The sincere philosopher is satisfied with the intuitive power, which raises his soul above the material things of this life, giving him an inceptive view of his present spiritual nature, which adheres to all purified spirits. But have we not all had those experiences? Yes. It is essential that we pass through the gross material; none can aspire to the purely intellectual without first having experiences in the lower spheres. Consequently, those who are benefited on that plane gradually emerge a step higher. After they reach an elevated position, above the present material one, they will comprehend why they were permitted to pass through that ordeal. The law of progress advances views founded upon facts, which become tangible to the investigator as he reaches the higher portals of spiritual progression. It is all mental power. This magnetic force which conveys to mortals the tangible facts, is the individualized life substance ; it strengthens the material organs of the physical body, giving power to the mental organs, through which the spirit manifests itself.

The more power you attract, the more power is concentrated, the more independent the spirit becomes. It is reasonable then to advise that knowledge of spiritual things, so called, which lie inert in the laws of nature, is only obtained through this life-force magnetism. It is the life substance of every living creature, both animal and human beings. We in spirit feel the deficiency of this power, especially if the intellectual faculties have been neglected. Progression advances step by step into that real, natural life. None can enjoy the true natural, unless they work out of the material ; by thus doing, they become loving, sympathetic, and charitable creatures, having a tendency to reach the good and omit the evil, wherever opportunities give them conditions.

Such is life, Brother S. You now have seen that which has made an impression on you. You, too, will comprehend intuitively why the material manifestations have no attractions for you. Your band is above that plane. Your calling is above that plane. Consequently, your spiritual inclinations and desires reach forth to the higher. The Nazarene said, "Ye have the poor always with you; but me ye have not always." The undeveloped you have at any time you desire them; being so much of the earth, they require the magnetic emanations of the earth, which gives them strength, and they are ever ready to manifest their power, often unobserved by mortals here. But the intellectually gifted and pure ye have not the power (to bring them to you at once), but they must be invoked through pure magnetic conditions. Let this be impressed upon all true seekers and sincere philosophers. True they will feel it themselves, even as you have felt it. Nevertheless, have charity for all.

God bless you! and remember the work we have before us is of no ordinary character. Could you see from our standpoint, you would not be surprised at our not making a more rapid progress. The misrepresentation of a personal deity, of Pagan forms of worship, which are all no more sanctioned than the misrepresentations of spiritual characters in the materializing *séances* which you attended.

Are not God and Christ misrepresented to millions of individuals? Yes; over two-thirds of the population are this day deceived by misrepresented spiritual ideas (coming) through sincere individuals. Think of it, and I will unfold many impressions.

The world at large is deceiving each other. And it is on this account we work. If you could view the conditions from our standpoint, you would think that our chances for success were as a drop of water in comparison to the sea. But we have hope, which gives us strength to work on. Work in the great cause of truth, and spiritual light will interblend and give the soul its development, to realize and comprehend the truest God, the Infinite Deity, and the mother of all productive power. This is the light, this is the hope, this is the power: we never weary. Good-day.

"Skywauke. Me come, chief. An honest medium never gets materialization; all who stand upon a low plane get benefit there."

Fifteenth Communication.

October 10, 1879.

HOW can fraud ever result in producing a benefit to mortals? was a question upon which my mind had been, and was dwelling upon when, sitting down to the *séance* table, Ben Haman announced himself as usual with, —

Good-morning, my son! we are happy to communicate this morning. I require some moments to collect my faculties; the nervous condition of the medium causes this. I will first refer to the interview you had at the materializing *séance* at ———.

The characteristic nature which the medium displayed, is not sanctioned by ourselves, consequently, we opened your eyes to the deception. I have told you before that she is a medium upon the trance order. Had she abided by the development of the trance power, she might have accomplished more good. But, being wrapped up too much in self and mammon, she forsook the holy and pure, threw them off as it were, and accepted the undeveloped, fraudulent influences of a lower plane.

The assuming of characters under spirit control, providing a truthful explanation is given of how it is produced, is sanctioned by the superior developed powers, and is often assisted by them. There are many minds which cannot accept the intellectual at first, but require tangible objects to make an impression, which is necessary. They, too, are also required to develop thought, and direct the attention to spiritual things. The A B C of spiritual development lies in the material surroundings of the individual. Consequently it is imparted through the cruder material and forms a tangibility, through which satisfaction is imparted to the searching mind.

These manifestations do a great deal of good upon that material plane. They are the phenomena for which the majority seek, and if conducted upon a pure, truthful plane work out good effects.

However, the majority of mediums allow themselves to become influenced by those sceptical influences that are brought to them by investigators. These very influences, being anxious to make an impression on their friends in the material, will impress the medium to give herself up to their designs; she being a negative, readily yields to their wishes. Procuring the material, she will apply it in such a manner upon her external body, and on other objects, necessary in producing the desired effect. Those influences throwing their magnetism over her, while imitating character after character with their magnetic power in connection with her will, can and do represent the character which they claim to be present.

In this wise, deception is practised upon the community. It is deception in one sense, and yet spirit influence in another. First the additional part which the medium performs; second, the assumption of the spiritual influences controlling, in personating a character which they are not, is the deceptive part of the manifestations. The medium is not entirely to blame for this; she subjects herself to those influences in her negative condition; she, being sensitive to every thought which is emitted from the spiritual influences in attendance, is therefore readily controlled by their designing will; in addition to which the material object, in making money and gaining notoriety, which to some minds is very gratifying. Taking all these things in consideration, the spiritual intelligence cannot change it.

We must have time. Time with proper conditions will gradually develop the human race. With the gradual development of the minds in mortal form, we shall be able to show them and to give them a clearer insight into the spiritual philosophy. You must learn to sift the pure from the dross. Those very manifestations, with their designing influences, in their tendency develop good effects. Out of the undeveloped material there develops, when properly applied, the most superior effects. The untutored mind must first learn the alphabet before it is able to spell a sentence. The sentences spelled out in an object convey a different meaning in reality to that of the single letter. Therefore from the crude material, the spiritual is developed. Particle after particle of the refined is converted into the more refined, and interblends through a chemical process, according to nature's laws, with the purest essence, which we apply for spiritual use in our spiritual spheres of progress.

There is no evil; there may be a wrong. Wrong committed through undeveloped organs will certainly be set right when the individual development realizes and recognizes the true course through conviction. This constitutes progression. If it were not for this undeveloped condition, there would be no need for development. If your organism was made perfect, so that your spirit could accomplish a perfection in every experience, there would be no progression made by you.

You must consider the undeveloped state of this planet itself. Mortals placed here to vegetate in the flesh, partake of all those crudamental particles, consequently mortals are given to the wrong more than to the right, more to the unundeveloped than to the developed. The undeveloped, when applied, benefits the material body, through which the material sense is gratified. When I say material sense, I mean the spirit in its undeveloped material state. There are thousands upon thousands who live to gratify the material appetite, the cravings of the material body. In such persons, the spirit interblends entirely with the soul propensities which enjoys the material experiences and conditions applied to it, and has no desire for the loftier aspirations of spiritual life.

Now for such persons those very material manifestations are beneficial. The pure essence of spiritual culture could not be imparted to them, could make no more impression on them than you can on a dumb brute.

Everything is presented from the spirit-world in a true light and for a good purpose. Time only will have power, as before stated, to change those conditions.

The philosopher has no interest in the alphabet. And so with yourselves, who have obtained a higher degree of knowledge, you cannot take much interest in the material manifestations.

Having received perfect instruction, and by careful observation, you have developed that sense, which many others are seeking to develop, called the sixth sense, or spiritual part of man ; the unfolding of which imparts a power to the perceptivity of your individuality.

When thoroughly interested, the spiritual guides impart knowledge which is information from the inner life, through and by which you become convinced of facts which exist in the spiritual laws of nature. That which you cannot grasp materially is all spirit. Mind is a spiritual essence, the production of which lies in nature's laws. Consequently it is matter refined and indestructible, though subject to changes. Consequently, I have told you, it is the duty of all who have attained the higher forms of development, to have charity for those who are struggling for light. Light is knowledge, and has a power to work out effects. Darkness is ignorance, and gropes its way carefully, and must have gleamings of light, the faintest ray of which will assist those groping their way into the light. And it is the duty of those who have obtained the power to work out effects in the light, to assist those still grovelling in darkness. Send them a ray of light, which is sympathy ; have patience with their prejudices, even with their arrogance, for they cannot bear the bright light at once. There are crooks and by-ways through which they must be led carefully, until they reach the gleam of light, in the brilliancy of which they will be assured that they are on the right road. Even as the mother has patience with the faltering babe in teaching it the first step, so the superior intellect must have patience, and with perseverance assist his fellow-man, in bringing him up and placing him in the right road of progress and of power.

Out of evil there developeth good. Evil, so called, is undeveloped good. If it were not so, there would be no outgrowing from the undeveloped into the spiritual state. That which seems deceptive to the most advanced investigator is but a physical display, assisted by undeveloped powers to work out good effects.

SIXTEENTH COMMUNICATION OF BEN HAMAN. — REINCAR-
NATION.

October 17, 1879.

GOD bless you, my son! We come with all the happiness I can bestow to say a few words about the ante-natal.

I have revealed to you a portion of the philosophy of reincarnation, being well aware of the fact that there are but few in the material who have advanced sufficiently to apply this knowledge with persistent and patient investigation.

You have now developed this power, through which you can receive and comprehend that mortals must live many lives in order to perfect themselves for the spiritual spheres.

"Verily I say unto you, unless a man be born again, he cannot enter the kingdom of heaven." This heaven, this summerland which Christ spoke of, lies far beyond this material sphere, and cannot be reached until the individual spirit has developed sufficient self-sustaining power.

Then again, "In my Father's house are many mansions. I go to prepare a place for you." Those mansions vary in degree; they are conditions applicable to the mortal nature of man, attainable according to his degree of unfoldment. Many there are who enter those mansions or degrees, and live centuries satisfied with the conditions or degrees they have attained on earth. Presently, on awakening to the reality, a desire to advance develops itself, and they find, in order to accomplish it, they must return and work out effectually experiences on this material plane. This material sphere being in close proximity with those conditions or mansions so called, they add and take according to the development of the spirit while in the material form. Many failures there are and have been in those experiences.

Immortals return with a desire to accomplish a purpose. If the organization of the material body is weak and diseased from too great an excess of material influences, which produce defective conditions, the body wastes and decays, the spirit returns, without having accomplished much in its desired experiences, and enters upon the same plane or sphere which it has occupied before.

Perseverance of the will, which has its marked effects upon the spirit while in the form, will cause them to return, oft times immediately, and with more successful effects.

That it is a general thing is demonstrated to the material senses of man by the difference in their development. Many in their youth are far superior to others in an advanced age; many there are who are far advanced spiritually, with the spiritual experiences by which their individuality is made perceptible to a close observer. Observing these conditions, so normal to the sense, you cannot help but see that where one perfects himself or herself, they are more sympathetic, more charitable to their fellow-men. The individualized spirit bears no arrogance, no malice to his fellow-man; all is harmony and love, concentrated with a tendency to assist through sympathy wherever he can.

Your own life has been a round of changes. Impressions which I tried to impart to you in your youth were thrown off, because you thought they were fancies of an unnatural character; and yet in their tendency they conveyed to you, in the form of development, the unfoldment of your inner nature.

It was not until you had passed through many changes and experiences that I was able to impress you in the light, to seek for the true material power, through which the spiritual could be imparted. Change after change. The restless spirit sought for the power through which this truth could be verified.

Eventually I brought you here. Through the channel of this magnetism I am now enabled to convey to you facts through which you will be enlightened, and by which the veil will be lifted; revealing to you the true causes, the effects of which you have always considered shrouded in mystery.

Passing by these changes I will first speak of your last and present one. With careful guarding I have guided you from the moment of material birth. And before this change it was I who sought your earthly parentage. Being endowed with large spiritual perceptiveness, I could penetrate the material, and saw in the material parents, father and mother, moral and intellectual gifts sustained by charitable purposes, from which I knew they would be enabled to produce good organizations and perfect souls.

Not all guides or guardians in spirit are developed up to this standard, consequently the many failures. If we can see clearly, we certainly can choose the more perfect organs for the perfecting of a soul.

I observed with carefulness your youthful training. There were some immoral impurities, which intercepted for the time being your development, which had to be permitted in order to bring about other effects. Mortals did censure you in their ignorance: they knew not why we often permit undeveloped effects to take place, in order to bring out the more perfect and good.

This was your experience at college, an experience you were compelled to pass through; without it your spiritual sympathetic nature never would have developed. Suffering, with its evil effects, is produced for a good purpose. (See note A at end of this Communication.)

There is but one great God, or principle rather, and he created both good and evil, which is developed and undeveloped. Man has been created to work out the effects of both. The undeveloped, being related more to his material organization, which is matter in an undeveloped state; he is drawn more to the material or to the undeveloped, and must, through many experiences, develop out of that condition to the more perfect.

This is the law of reincarnation: you are planted, the spiritual essence is planted in the material essences, and through the exertion in encountering those experiences you eventually perfect yourselves.

The infinite mind has created good and evil, and reigns supremely with intellectual power over the whole. The spiritual and intellectual are above in the purer atmosphere which surrounds this planet. The material and undeveloped are in the midst of you and your surroundings. There is but one great cause which produces those effects, and the sense of man, which is spirit combined with the material, must strive, through exertion of his will, to control the material, and to raise himself above it. The further he ascends above it, the more his comprehension reaches out into the spiritual; and through the potency of this great electric power with which he comes in contact, the stronger and more potent the will becomes.

In this wise, knowledge is obtained. Knowledge when obtained can be applied to controlling spiritual as well as material things. This is power so-called, and is only obtainable by those who have lived many lives in this material atmosphere.

Your material parents were moral and pure; striving to do their duty by their offspring, as near as they understood to be right, they performed the material functions necessary for the happiness of yourself. Their guides being in spiritual relation with myself, I frequently conveyed my ideas through the monitor of their impressiveness, instructing them what course to pursue with yourself, so that this life might not prove a failure.

You had large sympathy and love, and all the respect due to a dutiful offspring. However, your restless spirit was not satisfied. The experiences which were impressed upon you, you sought to realize. We found that in the professional avocation to which you had applied yourself with so much vanity, you could never accomplish or work out the effectual experiences. Consequently, we carried you into the forest, burying you from the many hurtful influences, excluding you entirely from the treacherous influences of undeveloped individuals. There in the deep-tangled woods, with the voice of the loved ones in their spiritual sympathy around you, and the voice of nature responding to your inner development, I found we could physically develop you for a good cause, the purpose of which is now being fulfilled.

A guardian in spirit, who will guide and protect the mortal from evil as near as he can, admitting only such suffering as may be essential for a good purpose, — in such a spiritual guardian's love there is something more than mere material affections, something more than that fictitious love which changes with the shift of the wind. This guardian love, this spiritual attention, is the love of a spiritual parent made so perfect through earthly ties at first.

And now since your spirit has unfolded, and can comprehend the gleams of light which I have imparted to you, and can be guided by the loving will of one who has striven to do his duty, may you work out in every sense the will, of him who ordained it, who stands highest of all. O my son, strive to realize that we are all workers for that great central Power. I am portraying to you this divine truth, through the assistance of some who are my superiors, and are doing my duty, and but assisting the great Father to accomplish and perfect his children, the human family.

This is why, when you went to see the Anderson medium, your mind was fixed upon the portrait of your father, your material parent. True, I impressed that affection upon you, which must and will remain even to eternity; but, through the interblending of my power, which claims its right from the more perfect source, I presented myself. My head and face conveyed to you through magnetic influence a feeling of love and admiration. I wished it to be so. That feeling developed thought after thought within your mind, until you have arrived at the very pinnacle of spiritual knowledge, and attained that which unites us closer in strength, to work out more effectually the great good to our fellow-man.

You are the material instrument through whom we can accomplish much good; and by thus giving yourself up, you are outgrowing the experience of the past, and fulfilling the mission assigned to you.

The relation of this spiritual attraction is very remote. It is not essential that I should pass through (i. e., relate) the different changes since its first development. Suffice it when I say, I was once your material father — not only once, but twice. The first impregnation of your spiritual identity was intrusted to my material care. Centuries after centuries have rolled on with their unmitigated changes.

You have conquered as a ruler, as many others have, with the iron wrath of a material brute. So much so, that in your last life you made very little progress, owing to the reproaches of those victims you held in bondage. As Archibald, you were stern and severe. I strove hard to guide you aright. I then, too, lived on earth, but the iron will of your positive nature could not be influenced by me. Consequently, you perished under the sword, — assassinated. That dates back before the birth of Christ. (See note B.)

However, you were Persian again. In that life, the second, was the first spark of your spiritual development. Having made so many failures, caused so much suffering, you were brought into the same atmosphere, with the same conditions to control, in order to test the ability of your individual development. When the remorse of a soul is so great, it is sure to throw itself back at once, to escape the tortures of influences that reproach it. Those tortures are called by the Catholics, purgatory. The prayers offered up in good faith, in the performance of high mass, frequently harmonize the influences, and relieve the spirit for the time being.

In your second life, I find you made a little more progress. I was attracted to you immediately after my death, and passed through changes with you, — experiences which were a benefit to me; and, as I gained power, I imparted assistance to you.

In the German life as Rozono, I determined to influence you against your own will. I knew it would be better for you. You were too material — too positive, and destroyed yourself. I met you in spirit. An understanding was had that you would produce certain conditions in the working-out of experiences, through the medium of another source, by becoming my material son again.

I immediately incarnated; found myself in the character of an Italian nobleman, Signior Rubenes, the sculptor. You were born with the same name and profession. I had no recollection of what had transpired in spirit between us, but I felt a sacred duty impressed upon me — that of having you educated. Being sincere and spiritual myself, having large individuality, I had you educated as a priest of the highest order, under the careful instruction of good Father Burno.

You were promoted to bishop, and from bishop to cardinal, Cardinal Lasseno. Your life proved a failure, by being destroyed through Borgia, who poisoned you with a ring while supping with him in the monastery of Saint Lucia. The times were very rebellious. Pope after pope was dethroned. You strove to ascend to the power of pope. Lucretia Borgia was in love with you. Borgia, her brother, was jealous of your ambition and destroyed you.

When entering spirit life I found you in a very weak state, being full of vengeance. You threw off a great deal of magnetic power. In that way you were injured, or injured yourself, nor would you listen to reason from me. You determined to avenge yourself, and came back to earth with a full desire to attain the power of pope, but failed.

Hovering around in the same atmosphere, you were directed and assisted to the accouchement of an humble peasant. Through the assistance of your spirit guides you entered upon a new life, much upon the same plane with the material surroundings of your previous life, excepting that your parents then were Romans — at least, the father. You were educated and trained in the Roman school of architecture, but being brought within political influences, you gave your attention in that way, and became involved in the rebellion of different nations.

You joined the ranks of artillery. Your energy, ambition, and revengeful spirit were displayed in the great battle of Buerns, in which General Litchera fell. Litchera was yourself. You displayed some noble feats there, from which good effects developed. Since then you have repeated yourself twice, once in France. Passing through a great deal of suffering, you came to spirit life humble and receptive.

After that, in the English character, in Queen Mary's time, you played a part as Burk. In the persecutions on account of religious dogmas you saved the lives of several who had been condemned by various acts and devices, through the spiritual assistance of myself and others. At the end of that life you committed a wrong. At the latter part of that life you were married to a young woman who confided greatly in you, but you contracted a love for another, and had her destroyed — instigated the murder. He who instigates a murder, who conceives it in his mind, is more a murderer than he who strikes the dagger to the heart, and the expiation of this crime you are now working out. Having good traits of character at that time, your spirit had attained knowledge which incited you to strive hard to accomplish good works, yet in assisting those you saved you caused others to be punished. Your spirit was yet in a very undeveloped state, and you died of grief, broken-hearted for the wrong act against your physical conjugal.

You lived in spirit with me numbers and numbers of years, progressed in many things, enjoyed the bliss of the spiritual life. You sought the object of your love, your soul's affinity, which can only be obtained through progression. You might have remained but for your attraction for an affinity in a higher sphere.

This affinity is with you. She assists me with your daily experiences, not always, but gives you strength when she comes, understanding the laws which assist the immortal soul to happiness through progression. You were willing to take upon yourself the physical cross, with its material experiences, and, with faith in your future happiness, you returned to this life; the rest you know.

Any questions to ask? I was too much astounded to ask any.

I want you to understand that we are co-workers. My love is the outpouring of the great Infinite Creator's. You are now ready to understand it.

You have a pure nature, which I have been instrumental in unfolding, and will be enabled to guide *you* aright, and assist you to impart to others by impregnating your magnetism in their system. A pure nature is spiritual; an impure nature is material. Abide by that which is good and pure. You cannot do otherwise. You are conscientious, true, and sincere, and I thank the All Infinite Power for giving me strength to unfold your nature, and lead you up higher, where spiritual purity interblends with your thoughts. Abide with the pure, with the good in heart, for they shall see and enjoy the happiness of the summer spheres.

God bless you, my son! and may his protecting care and love ever interblend with your soul, as it does with us. Amen.

NOTE B. — On the advice of Mrs. Watson I called on a Mrs. Manly of Erie, Penn., for a sitting. She handed me some eight pages of note-paper covered with writing of such an allegorical character that I could make nothing out of it. Years afterwards mentioning the same to Mrs. Glading she advised me to send it (I had only a copy) to Dr. Cooper of Bellfountain, Ohio, for a translation. He returned it saying, "I do not know whether you believe in reincarnation or not, but I am impressed that you were an Eastern potentate in a former life — 'a lover of songs.' You were an admirer of Ovid, a contemporary with you."

NOTE A. — In 1838 I received a summons to appear before the faculty of Jefferson College, Pennsylvania. I was charged with being the wildest boy at college, going on an occasional spree, and neglecting my regular studies, and was suspended from college. I was then in my eighteenth year. I immediately wrote a long letter to my father, palliating my conduct, and asking for money to meet some of the debts I had contracted, intending upon receipt of the money to take it and hide myself in the far West, as, when he would realize the total amount of the indebtedness I had contracted, he would be justly incensed and angry with me. Just as I was about to mail the letter, as I stood on the post-office porch, I received a letter with a black seal — it announced the death of that father!

Was it necessary for a supernal power to intervene, and at the expense of the life of that father to snatch me from destruction? was a thought which haunted me for years. How will my poor mother bear the double infliction of father's death and my disgrace? The thought led me to ask the faculty to withhold a notice of their action from my mother. Returning to my mother's now desolate home, who with meagre means was left with a large family of small children on her hands, I strove hard to assist her in fighting the wolf from the door. I ate many a plate of mush, salted with tears of regret that I had been the cause of loosing her stay and support. A confession never before made to mortals, but alluded to in the foregoing, when speaking of "your experience at college."

SEVENTEENTH COMMUNICATION OF BEN HAMAN.

October 31, 1879.

ARCHIBALD I., same as Archilaus, was before Christ, nearing the birth of Christ during the reign of Herod.

If mankind go about development, they will find that man . . . must perfect himself through experiences.

The histories I have given you of all those lives, were given merely to convince you of this fact that, there are changes in spirit life as well as in the material, not that you derive any material benefit from it. Oh, no; in purpose it is purely spiritual. It has aroused that dreamy nature of yours into consciousness, through which you realize why you live, and to what purpose you can make this life an advantage, not only for yourself but for others also.

As before stated, through the development of those perceptive organs of yours you become more impressive; and I will in future be enabled to impress upon you with identical firmness the true character of the ante-natal lives which you have passed through. The sufferings through failures have also made their impression on you. Now that this life is more perfect than any of the others ever were, you will be enabled through the assistance of myself and others to accomplish the work for which you returned, and work out the mission urged upon you.

Change after change takes place in this material life, likewise in the spiritual. We are constantly working, and through the energetic power of our wills we impart assistance to mortals here. Every one imparts according to his degree of development. In your workshops you have inventors, in your seminaries you have philosophers, the laboring man has his attractions in that sphere to which his development corresponds. The philosophic draw the intellectual to their assistance, etc.

But there is a time when we desire to perfectly accomplish our work in order that we may leave earth's sphere and locate permanently with those minds with whom we interblend.

You have now had many experiences; your desire has naturally developed sufficient in strength, the will of which acts as a potency in locating yourself.

This we desire to accomplish. Many centuries have passed. Your spirit is very old, and the many and various experiences have individualized you sufficiently, so that your strength is drawn from the reservoir of nature. The fountain of purity which has developed this individuality within you, has given you strength to throw off the iron shackles of dogmatic creeds, and freed you from all material attractions and interests.

Not until a mind liberates itself from those material errors can it comprehend the intellectual power which is imparted through this fountain of life, the magnetic-electric power, which emanates from the great Creator. The electric, which is the creative power and positive force, impregnates the magnetic and more negative force, the two interblend as one and produce the growth of vegetation which emanates from the soil of this globe; likewise the semen of man, which contains the life-germ of electric power, impregnates the female ovary, which is the negative-magnetic power, the two elements interblending constitute life ; animal life on a higher plane.

Man is a composition of the various elements; there is not

one within the mineral or vegetable kingdom which the human body does not contain. It is composed of a variety of elements, in particles or germs. When the physical body becomes deficient or weak there is a lack of one or two or more of these elements; consequently suffering sets in, and the body becomes weakened, and unless restored by external applications or substitutes, it must continue to lose. One after the other are thrown off, and return to the elements through the exhalation of the porous system. You breathe, not only through the nostrils, but through numerous cells, which are in constant activity, throwing off the impurities of the body; these are drawn in through inhalation, and again thrown off to the elements, to return again through a purified process of this magnetic law.

Oxygen contains the purest electric force. Hydrogen gives the magnetic force. The two interblend with much power, and benefit the animal kingdom. One of these alone is too positive, and cannot give the full benefit which the human system requires. When the soul leaves the body along with the spirit, life is extinct. Then oxygen and hydrogen are of no avail. Then the electric-magnetic power acts in a different manner: instead of imparting life, it consumes it, disintegrates and carries off the whole of the body in a vapory form; being consumed, it returns to the elements from which it was composed. Every particle, though buried out of sight within the soil, is attracted to that of which it was composed; change after change in various forms take place.

This, man must consider the great reservoir of nature, the electric-magnetic power of which I would be able to give you a full description in its pure state, both before it impregnates your atmosphere and after, if the medium will comply with the requests now appealed to her.

There are laws in nature which would be of great benefit to the intellectual mind if it comprehended them, or would make them a study. There is but a tithe of knowledge imparted from the great spiritual source, and there are still, at the present day, as many souls annihilated as there were thousands of years ago. Science constitutes progress; knowledge is power, and power constitutes the spiritual development. The human family will now learn, through the spiritual development, that they must perfect themselves here in knowledge, and can attain only through experience that happiness which the spirit craves, but which none can fully realize until they have developed or advanced out of the earth's sphere.

For this reason I have given you the ante-natal parts' of your lives. You may well say it lies with the past. But the spirit buries nothing. Out of the material sight it may be, out of the material mind, or the mind while living in the material body; but when the spirit enters upon a new life, this life of activity, it unfolds itself gradually, and the energetic nature of the spirit will again perceive and comprehend according to the desire, according to the will and nature of the individual.

Just so the unfoldment of the mind in recognizing the past, which, in a dreamy condition at first, cannot realize or comprehend perfectly that which your orthodox ministers call a union in heaven. Spiritual teachers err there. Those unions in heaven do take place in the spiritual spheres, but not in reality, as they claim and portray them to mortals. Many come and seek their friends, provided they have individuality sufficiently developed to realize that they have friends or relatives here. They may know them, if they are drawn magnetically to them; otherwise they do not.

It is for this reason that spiritual-magnetic circles should be holden with perseverance, so that men and women can learn the laws which control the universe through the positive force, magnetic and electric; when this can be demonstrated, man will gradually realize, through the development of his physical organs, the true source from which happiness is obtained.

It is by being led the wrong way, guided in the same manner his progenitors were guided, that this dogmatic doctrine and error, soul salvation, has blighted his life, as it has previously that of thousands of others. Through disappointments and errors, the spirit lives and returns, and lives again, with little or no better success.

Not until the uprooting of this evil error, which men and women have clung to with great tenacity, even to desperation, can they make spiritual progress. Incited as it is, this dogmatic error conveys to it a hopeful and trusting confidence; and when it enters spirit-life, it finds but little benefit from its effects. In darkness, regret and disappointment develop sorrow, with many in an undeveloped state a feeling of revenge; and more often they are the first to take advantage of an opportunity, and immediately reincarnate.

This is why you have at the present so many materialists. They are mostly individuals who have through some great disappointment thrown themselves back to work out their vengeance against the dogmatic doctrine of soul salvation.

Be hopeful, and learn to realize the individuality which your soul has attained through this development. This cannot be revealed to all. The ignorant herd must continue with the surging mass, who are striving to gain their salvation through sectarian creeds. Not until they realize disappointment in spirit, not until they return with the impression it makes upon all truthful, energetic minds, — not until then, I say, will they be enabled to comprehend the true source of happiness. True enough, it lies within the reach of all, but they who cannot grasp it, certainly cannot be benefited through its subilme power.

He who always looks upon the dark can never see the light.

October 31, 1879.

UPON asking for medical advice for my wife, who at the time was somewhat indisposed, B. H. said, "Don't fear or have uneasiness. I think we can arrange the domestic surroundings. The mother who performs or fills such a large mission in the household, is somewhat crushed in spirit and physically debilitated. We have directed our attention upon her. We must impart proper conditions, that she may yet remain in the bosom of her family. True, the ante-natal germ is trying hard to develop itself within her system; but with proper remedies, along with rest and care, she will be able to baffle the disease. She has positive will-power, which is a great boom to her physical health. Be hopeful, that which you desire the most will surely be worked upon; in accomplishing those purposes, you will be enabled to overcome those material defects which have so long obstructed your way to spiritual progression. Gradually the unfolding organs of the material body feel the consoling effect, which this healing band imparts to you, and through this power you are enabled to assist those loved ones intrusted to your care. Through this vital power you have given strength to, and prolonged the life of the dear mother. She has benefited largely from your magnetism, and can still be benefited, now more than ever. The magnetic unfolding of your physical organs imparts to her the vital life, through and by which she has been sustained these many years, and also imparts to the little ones alike the same. The elder youth, who is absent at present, misses this magnetic band and suffers in consequence thereof. We will establish a battery to convey the magnetism of yourself to him (at Evanston, Ill.), which is highly essential and must be attended to with care and strict attention on your part. Direct your thoughts to him every morning before arising from your bed. Your thoughts must be directed upon his head. In this wise the magnetic current will penetrate him through; no matter where he may be he will become stronger and not suffer from this debility.

EIGHTEENTH COMMUNICATION OF BEN HAMAN.

November 14, 1879.

MIND is an essence which cannot be destroyed, and requires material aid to assist in its development. Being an essence highly refined, constituted of forces that hold in their possession the power of oxygen and hydrogen, electric and magnetic elements combined, it presents itself as all gaseous forms do. Yet through this process of development it becomes inert in the human body, because the human body being composed of a combination of elements, vegetable and mineral particles, the essence of spirit-material comes in contact with every kind. Through its development it partakes of these different elements. They impart strength to the spirit through the development and growth of the body. The body being matter destructible nevertheless contains all those elements so essential to the strength of the spirit. If the body is weak and diseased, it does not impart to the spirit any nourishment, hence the spirit feels the deficiency and is unable to work out effectually its natural experiences.

This law proves itself in those mortals who have diseased physical bodies; they have no energy, no will, and become depressed and irritable. Health and strength of the physical body are essential. All intellectual minds should observe this, and pay strict attention to the organic development of the material body.

By observation you will see that for all who perform mental labor where mind is more employed than material organs, more animal food is essential. Why? simply because the spirit must be nourished by the body. The body must feed the mind. Mind extracts the essences of the body. There are three divisions of the food; namely, that which goes to the spirit, the refined, that which is imparted to the blood; and the cruder waste, which is thrown off through fecal discharges.

This law is not yet understood. As a general thing, mortals do not realize that by neglecting or abusing the material body they are sinning against the spirit. For, as before stated, the spirit depends solely upon this material body for sustenance and strength. Much can be added, and a great deal taken away, by a neglect of this law. Bright intellect can be developed; mind can be cultivated if the material body performs its natural functions. No one should, under any consideration, neglect the material body; every condition necessary to its growth, health, and strength should be complied with. THIS should be the first lesson taught to the child, and firmly impressed upon his or her mind as a religious duty; for without the material there can be no advance of the spiritual, and without the spiritual the material would perish, for it would have no life.

Mind when disembodied, when freed from these material substances, is powerful. Material experiences are essential for its growth in this power. The soul, which partakes of the whole of the second form of essenic development in the body, adheres to the spirit. The blood in these material organs promotes the growth and is the life of the material body.

Spirit being essence divine, the formation of which I have already explained, soul, which is electric life, material, which is animal life, together constitute man. The electric maintains the material, for without the electric force there could be no material; this element gives vitality and activity which constitute life. This power inert within the body through material development imparts the substance to the spirit, which develops its power and gives it strength to work out material effects and spirit as one. In this wise the soul, while encased within the physical body, imparts to the spirit the conditions necessary for the development of individuality.

At the death of the material body, when the cruder matter is thrown off, the soul unites itself with the spirit, and the two interblend as one. The soul is then the envelope of the spirit, the external ; the spiritual intellect controls the whole, even as it controlled the material whole or body, but having more power to produce effects upon the elements, in the positive force of which it now has full control.

But this power can only be attained through material experiences, which impart power towards its development. Experience after experience is necessary for cultivating the spirit's growth. You require soil in which to plant seed. The seed could not expand and develop without the material soil; even so the spirit essence must be planted within the body, and the body develops the soul by partaking of solid substances which are produced from the soil, equalizing its nourishment, drawing from the elements the mineral, and from the soil the vegetable, and grows according to its adaptation and composition. If the germ of disease is imparted to the fetus it cannot develop the same strength and vitality that it would if that germ had been omitted.

The rising generation should make this a study. Sexual intercourse for the production of offspring should not be indulged in unless the bodies are healthy and vigorous. Nor should anything of the kind ever be permitted where the natures of the individuals are not opposite. Two dispositions that are mentally alike should never unite in the bands of wedlock, for the organic substances which develop the fetus are in similarity the same, and permit of no variation of the elements required for the production. Children produced from such parents have not the organs, the phrenological organs, thoroughly developed. They are more or less indolent in nature, devoid of energy, and subject to carelessness.

All depends on organization for future progress, material success, and spiritual culture. This should be looked to by all who contemplate matrimony. For much happiness could be attained, and much suffering and sorrow be avoided, by strictly observing this inert law.

If the human race would strive to acquaint itself with proper information in regard to reproduction, if it would but give one-third more of its attention to perfecting its offspring, there would not be so much degradation and corruption among them. I tell you, mortals can and have produced Gods.

The spirit that awaits incarnation, if he is intellectual, and desires to make an intellectual or spiritual experience in this material world, will investigate closely, and inform himself correctly of the organization and spiritual nature of the parents whom he has chosen.

Why do those persons who are brought up with very little of this world's goods produce the best, and often the most intellectual children?

Because living a simple life, complying with the natural laws of nature, and living on the plainer productions of the soil, more natural and more in accord with the material body, their physical organs contain the purer elements, and consequently produce healthy offspring, who, in their simplicity and unobtrusiveness, are easier controlled through spiritual impression.

You will find, through investigation, that they who have too many of this material world's goods become neglectful of their spiritual duty; they forget that which forms the principle part of happiness; viz., the unfolding of the spirit. Living a luxurious life, giving all to the material, every craving desire of the material body of any nature they gratify.

By thus doing, they weaken and abuse the body; becoming devoid of the even balanced elements, which should exist in its organization and consequent power, it fails in health. In this wise it suffers. Nature, in her laws, deals out fearful retribution for such violations. All is harmony in the laws of nature. Every mortal born attracts the same elements, but man with his undeveloped nature chooses the cruder material always, because it is more pleasing to the senses, and often does not realize the error until too late to remedy, then he passes out.

The spirit, having made no experience whatever, regrets the folly of his course; if sufficiently developed, it will seek to return immediately. But many times there are obstacles thrown in its way. He must and does abide his time in spirit life. Sometimes, according to his development, he works out his growth here in spirit life by coming in contact with earth; and if he has proper conditions given him, he can accomplish his purpose. He must have the material substance, which is matter refined, to give him strength.

Spirits draw heavily from mortal bodies; the food you prepare they partake of. Your spirit friends dine with you many times, and you know it not, unless you are clairvoyant and can see them with your spiritual eye. They partake of the aroma of all material substances. That which evaporates is the substance which nourishes the spiritual souls that surround you.

Even the infant that passes out prematurely is brought to the mother daily, and partakes of her magnetism, which gives it strength, and develops its soul growth. The infant grows to maturity, but it could never do so without the material magnetism. This magnetism is as essential to its growth as your material substances are to yours. All who have passed out prematurely must inevitably return; those who are more advanced, if they are self-sustaining, return to work out experiences; the little ones are conveyed here to the parent stem to draw the life substance, which is magnetism, and assists in developing its growth.

This philosophy, when more thoroughly comprehended (we do not expect it to be thoroughly comprehended for many centuries), will enable mortals to develop more purity of character, more conscientiousness, and their duty toward each other will be better understood.

Infants grow in spirit life with matronic care from the fifth sphere, where there are matrons and maidens who perform the duty of instructing and cultivating them. All this care is assigned to females; they, being spiritually adapted, perform this duty with love and sympathy. The maiden must have the experiences of a mother. She passes through every experience that a mother in the material body passes through upon the higher order. Those little ones that are reared in the fifth sphere are sent to the earth daily; they are sent in circles, with proper care, and with magnetic conditions, which are always regulated by their spiritual guides. They receive from the material, they must have material experiences. And they are the guardians of many of earth's children. A lesson: Even as they assist you, even so should you assist each other in the material. The law of charity, the philanthropic development, and the generous principles are the attributes of the fifth sphere.

NINETEENTH COMMUNICATION OF BEN HAMAN.

November 27, 1879.

ELECTRICITY, or material magnetism, furnishes strength and substance for the soul's growth, which is the spirit body, the same as the material body requires solid substances combined with elementary fluids which are drawn from the atmosphere; those same fluids are impregnated in the material magnetism. It is a higher substance, containing oxygen and hydrogen combined with electric fluids. Those three elements impart substances for the growth of material bodies. As before stated, the spirit, while in the material body, obtains its substance from the blood; the blood being inoculated with those essences which add largely to the strength and vitality of the material body. Nevertheless, when separated from the material body the soul is an identical substance, which interblends with the elements, but is more refined than any solid substance which you have here in the material. It is lighter and more ethereal than your atmosphere, being a compounded element, the very essence of the separate forces which in uniting purify themselves, and produce a more ethereal body; it attracts immediately, draws as a magnet does steel.

This magnetism impregnates the spirit body, gives it a more material aspect; holding itself within this magnetism for a certain length of time, it becomes electrified, the same as you may be by a shock from an electric battery. Children, therefore, who have to grow and develop to maturity, are brought in contact with this material magnetism, that they may receive the proper conditions, and inhale the magnetism, which imparts to them vital power or physical strength. They are not permitted to remain long at a time; there is a certain portion necessary every day, the same as with yourselves; you must every day have fresh air, and if you do not have it, you suffer, becoming weak and debilitated.

Nor is this requisite for children alone, but adults, young and elder ones also, require this material magnetism. Not as long a period to all; but that depends upon the spiritual nature of the individual. If the soul is very material, it requires more material assistance. What we mean by material, is when the physical body is given to gross desires, if there is more attention paid to the material than to the spiritual, and every passion of the soul is gratified with sensual and gross desires, then the material body becomes saturated with the cruder parts of the electric elements. For be it clearly understood, that the body is nourished by the essences which are extracted from the solid food. Those essences, in the form of gases, permeate the blood, and if there is too much of one kind of food taken, that becomes an overbalanced power, and produces inharmonious effects in the blood, arousing passions, and not unfrequently disordering the whole system. The brain being the base of the physical body, those essences in their evolutionary growth stimulate that organ, and produce various diseases, when not in harmony with each other. They must interblend in equal proportion to each atom; they then develop a regular circulation, and add beneficial effects for the growth of the soul.

The spirit is many times controlled by the material propensity. The majority of human beings are more likely to be controlled by the material desires of the physical body which germinate from the soul, which is more animal, and is drawn to the material being; fed and nourished by the material, it is essentially material.

Therefore, humanity should learn the laws of nature, and learn that by cultivating the physical appetite, by abstaining from the grosser material, they impart a more perfect essence to the soul-growth. The soul imparts the essence refined to the spirit, which in its action stimulates and develops intellect.

This philosophy is very deep; the analysis of it in a perfect way would produce a volume in itself, but we must begin at the lower. Our object is to teach mankind to know themselves, and learn the anatomy of their physical bodies; then by understanding the formation of themselves, they will be enabled to realize the essentiality of cultivating the physical body, in order to perfect the soul and spirit.

The intellectual require assistance in development, and receive it through the channel of the soul, which is the monitor that replenishes the vital power of the spirit. When in a crude, material body which is given largely to the use of stimulants containing more gaseous substances, especially in liquid form, they inflate the soul, and make it weak, without any solidity whatever.

When such a soul enters spirit-life, it is necessarily drawn to the material, for the purpose of nourishing itself, more often from the same substances which it draws from the elements surrounding the individuals who are given to the use of stimulants; they scent it, the same as a hound does the magnetism of his master. Care should be taken that this law be generally understood, for many times those weak, debilitated creatures consume individual bodies by goading them on to excessive drink, feasting off the emanation of the highly charged and poisonous vapors which are thrown off in the respirations of their diseased bodies.

When such an individual passes over, they are mere nonentities. The soul in its single separate fluidic state can take no form; there being but one elementary atom, the other two being consumed through the influences of those beings, the spirit then seeks a body, and will take the very first opportunity to reincarnate.

Rarely ever is there a spirit which enters this life perfect in the formation of the soul; there is a deficiency of either one or the other of those elements, — oxygen, hydrogen, or electric magnetism. They must essentially perfect that body, and are drawn to your earth for that purpose. The most of them are put under treatment immediately. Experienced spirits, who are well-informed, take them in charge. They are nursed and carried hither and thither until strength is restored. Medicines are rarely ever resorted to in this treatment. They depend principally upon the manipulating power of material magnetism, and in time, with proper instructions from the physicians who have them in charge, they are enabled to cultivate the will, the strength of which enables them to exercise power over themselves, and learn to use the spiritual will in controlling such objects as are necessary for their own development.

Many of them, yes thousands of them, are brought to old mother earth without seeing or realizing their condition. It all lies in development; and those who are too weak to develop their faculties are left in a position in the spiritual sphere where they locate, the soul or spirit body not developing. For its development depends entirely upon the will of the spirit. And if there is too little will-force, there can be no soul-growth, and consequently annihilation consumes the soul, or, in other words, the soul is annihilated, wastes away in vapor, and the spirit is guided to take its course in another material experience. The individuality of the spirit is only attained through material experiences; and not until it has developed a certain degree of will-power can it accomplish anything toward its individuality.

All depends upon the development of this force. The magno-electric, which controls the whole physical body, is will-force. Intelligence is the magnetic. The electric is the positive. The magnetic is the intelligence. The electric is the positive and is the will, and through the electric the magnetic is assisted, they interblend and are one. The positive assists the negative; this is spiritual force, so called, and after disembodying itself from the material it controls all material.

If it has attained sufficient power through material experiences, it will be able to cultivate and perfect the soul, its body; but if not, it retraces and tries another and still another, until sufficient force is attained by which it is enabled to control the spiritual. Out of the material emanations of your planet, spirits are enabled to produce and manufacture objects which are as tangible to them as your material is to yourselves in the material.

This power, which is so potent in its attributes, must yield flexible to the will that the spirit may design; and if the power is not sufficiently developed, it cannot be controlled by the potent will. Knowledge is power when acted upon by the will; it is drawn in and controlled, as a solid substance yields to the flexible touch of the material hand. In this wise, the spirits of men and women become creators, gods as it were, endowed with the sublimest forces of nature's laws, and he or she who desires to outgrow the material experiences, can, through the exertion of the will, command spiritual forces and they will yield to their design.

The immortalized spirit becomes godlike in its attributes, and can attract all that is beautiful to the sense and all that can perfect its happiness.

Mind you, it lies in the individual's power to make himself or herself happy in this life, as well as in the spiritual. In the spiritual it is glorified by the development of the will-power. None need to suffer in this material life. The all-wise Creator has imparted alike to one and all the attributes through which the spirit develops.

True enough, experiences alone on this material planet enable the intellectual positive mind to outgrow the sensual and undeveloped. The pure and progressive spirit while encased within the material organs, should inform itself that intellect can accomplish nothing without will-force. Will-force constitutes the highest, and many times material effects are attained, if used in a proper direction. And more often if it stands alone, unsustained by intelligence, it follows out its material wrath which causes much suffering and sorrow. Such a course never benefits the spirit, but acts directly opposite, chaining it to the material, until such wrathful effects are worked out through good pursuits.

But where will-force and intelligence interblend, where the intellectual negative is assisted by the firm positive, man can and does make his home harmonious and beautiful. He locates where he feels the aspirations of his soul ascending to the realms of the cherubs, where ethereal expressions are sent to cheer him and assist him, where sublime happiness, peace, and contentment ever unite in harmony and love. No suffering, no sorrow, can reach him in that far distant sphere. It is only the desire of your own individual development that attracts you to such a locality.

Dear Readers, — It is the duty of all to pay strict attention to the cultivation of the material body, abstaining from all things which stimulate the passions, holding them under the spiritual control of the individual will. Then you will be imparting strength to the soul, and the soul will stimulate the spirit, so that your earthly pursuits and experiences will be beneficial to yourselves. Ever remember that you can make your heaven through the working out of those experiences. You can make that heaven whatever you desire, a sublimated sphere of happiness, or a hades of misery.

Men and women must strive to elevate themselves. They can only do so by working out good effects. If their purpose be to benefit each other, they will develop the germ of charity. They must strive to throw off the material shackles of selfishness which they have nursed so long with disappointed hopes. They must unite in sympathy with each other. They must extend the hand of fellowship, and especially he who has attained a certain degree of individuality, it is his or her duty to strive to comprehend that the true way to progress is to assist his fellow-being in the same path.

Nothing is more cheering to the spirit when it enters upon this natural life, than to look back to earth and receive the reflections of those whom he has befriended. This is self-elevation, this adds to the aggrandizement of the spirit, and inspires it with a feeling of love and sympathy for all, no matter how low. True, you cannot assimilate with them, but you can befriend and relieve their suffering, which adds to your self-sustenance, and it is only when you are enabled to assist others that you assist yourself, and through the merits of your own exertions you save yourself. This is the doctrine or philosophy of Spiritualism, so called. Spiritual elevation, I term it, and soul growth, for through the growth of the soul the spirit elevates itself. The spirit depends on the soul while in the body, but when disembodied the soul depends upon the spirit.

There can be no happiness or contentment, until this beautiful philosophy, this divine truth, is better understood. Through the teachings of those superior beings who are so deeply interested with you mortals on this old mother earth, sending their reflections through expressions to you; through the ever extended care of those loving ones who interest themselves so much for your spiritual happiness, the human family must, and will, progress. The pure expressions of love, virtue, and sympathy of the guides will impregnate in time the spiritual nature of mortals, so that they can realize and comprehend the true course to happiness.

TWENTIETH COMMUNICATION OF BEN HAMAN. — RECOGNITION OF FRIENDS IN THE SPIRIT SPHERES.

December 5, 1879.

MANY question whether they will know their loved ones when they enter spirit-life, children having outgrown their identity, parents fear that they may not recognize them. The magnetic link of attraction can never be severed. While the parents are in the physical body their children are drawn to them for sustenance. As before stated, the parents impart the proper essences for soul growth, and their children naturally feel and know their spiritual powers and the true benefit their magnetism imparts to them. Spirit children are more attracted and attached to their material parents than their physical offspring are. Unclouded minds that penetrate earthly surroundings can see clearer and comprehend more distinctly the material surrounding of the individual. So these little ones, growing up as they do under the fostering care of spiritual matrons, are brought in close sympathy with every thought, with every feeling, of the material parents; and this attraction holds so firm in spiritual relation that it cannot be changed. The minds of the parents become inert, as it were, while the mind of the infant youth or maiden reflects, turns back to the mother; she having the larger portion (of magnetism) to apply, which you observe in the material care and soul interest she takes in her infant, or offspring. Every thought conveys to the child a magnetic strength from the fountain of her vitality. Just as she imparts in its fetal development strength and growth, so she imparts in its natural material state not only in food, of which it partakes, but in her very atmosphere which conveys strength and vitality to its growth.

If you observe many times when a child becomes restless and wails for relief, the mother's soothing-magnetic touch dispels the pain and soothes it to rest. Again, not only does this magnetism impart vitality and strength, but it impresses their characteristic development according to the will of the matron.

Care should be taken in the rearing of infants (and it should be known by all) that they should be placed in an atmosphere where pure thoughts with virtuous surroundings permit the pure and most developed spiritual influences to attend and assist them.

This magnetic link which unites you so closely to the material, is certainly more effectual in the spiritual; for, laying aside all temptations and evil influences that work with so much potency in the material the spirit in its sublimer body can work with more effect and unite itself in closer sympathy with those who assist them in the material. By this magnetic chord of attraction parents will know their children, sisters will recognize each other, brothers will unite and vie with each other.

This law of attraction interblends with mortals in their material life, and many years of separation frequently work upon the mental capacities of their perceptiveness, estranging them, as it were, through forgetfulness, from those loved ones who have passed over, yet unknowingly do they convey material assistance, which is drawn from the emanations of their physical respiration.

There are different attractions. Parents may have six or seven offspring and not more than one or two are spiritually allied to them, and oftentimes out of lesser numbers there are none; but they are given to them to cultivate and assist them in having material experiences, which is a mission assigned to the parents, and the better they comply with every condition necessary for their offsprings' advancement and development in body and spirit, the more power and strength are bestowed upon themselves.

Every parent has a mission to fulfil in the rearing of souls and preparing them for higher spheres. This work, which is so practical to many, is entirely neglected by others, being largely dependent upon the experiences parents may have had.

Care should be taken that no restringent force be exercised, and that no dogmatic ideas be impressed upon the child. Their observation should be carefully directed to the natural philosophy in nature's laws and the God principle of the universe. Careful teachings of spiritual knowledge, and the identical power in connection with it, constitute the school in which the developing mind or spirit should be instructed. It will teach them to cherish the truth, to cultivate purity of character and sympathy of mind; it will impart naturally to the spiritual nature of mortals an aversion to wrong, and make them strive to practise with energy and will generous, sympathetic feelings for their fellow-men.

When this philosophy is generally understood, there will be a cessation of evil and of wrong-doing. When a mortal realizes that every wrong act, whether committed against his fellow-men or against himself, reflects upon himself, and that he must carry the burden of its weight, in this life as well as the after-life, he will strive to practise the teachings of the old philosophers embodied in the golden rule of the Christians — Do unto others as ye would others should do unto you.

Christ, the Reformer, tried very hard to initiate this rule among the Scribes and Pharisees; but owing to the ignorance of that day, and the predominating power of the Israelitish priestcraft, he was bitterly opposed, and his moral teachings were for a time crushed into oblivion. Premature as his teachings were in that day, they impregnated the very soil and atmosphere in which he lived. I have told you that thoughts are potent, and that there is nothing lost, not even a thought.

Thoughts, like expressions, convey magnetic power, and often impress the individuals for whom they are intended; no matter how far away the individual may be, distance does not decrease their power. So with the influence of this Reformer; the magnetism of his being, which he cultivated, the thoughts which were inspired by spiritual influences, thrown off in reflections, penetrated the soil as well as the atmosphere; the result was that more charitable ideas permeated the atmosphere, and more reasonable natures were reared within it. And thus it has been handed down from generation to generation through nineteen hundred years.

But what good has been accomplished by it? There has been in those nineteen centuries as much bloodshed, as much antagonism, and as much variance of opinion, as in the ages prior to that time when pagan ideas held full control.

The reason of this inharmony and variance of opinions is to be found in the erroneous ideas which the different sects took up, developed, and taught as divine truth, having originated, as they claim, with the great Creator, incarnated in a Saviour called the Nazarene or Christ, and conveyed to earth for the sole purpose of developing the human race.

This erroneous idea is all undeveloped truth. Truth in this wise : that the divine Creator created the spirit that incarnated in the body of Christ; that Christ strove to teach the truth; that he complied with every condition necessary for his spiritual guides to work out their purposes ; that he set noble examples by his honesty and by his purity of character, and that his whole desire was to benefit those who sought him with sincerity.

In this wise, the teachings of Christ and the present dispensation of spiritual development co-resemble and interblend with the divine truth, which the Creator designed in the very laws of nature ; and they must and will eventually develop, purify, and harmonize the human race.

The antagonisms which have also developed themselves out of the teachings of Christ have been caused by the conflicting ideas of the remote races in that day. I have told you that there is nothing lost : magnetism is indestructible, and every mortal who has lived on this earth has left a portion of his magnetism imbedded in the elements, as well as in the soil. This magnetism is applied to the material development of another body. I have told you that bodies growing in the material partake of substances in the atmosphere, which add to their material growth the same as to the growth of their spirits. Solid food does not furnish the whole substance for growth ; magnetic electric portions are just as essential. Now, drawing in this magnetism, which has been planted in the soil, individuals feel in their nature the effect. Eating of the products of this soil, it imparts a development of organic life. These organs are formed in the likeness of their progenitors ; they deviate but little from the parental germ, consequently they see or comprehend but little more than their forefathers or progenitors did.

By spiritual aid from intellectual spheres they are assisted.

They cannot be approached by superior beings at once, on account of the antagonisms which lie imbedded in the surroundings of the individual; but they receive assistance through reflections conveyed to them by impressions. In this wise they are benefited, and are guided to do generous acts.

Only through repeated changes of this magnetic electric power will the human race develop out of antagonism, jealousy, and bigotry. The very essences must first be purified. For as you have lived so the body dies. At the annihilation of the material body all the particles of its finer qualities go to the various elements; the cruder material returns to the soil. That, too, passes through chemical changes, which interblend with the soil, and return in a different form through vegetation, fruit and forest trees, the lower grade of animals subsisting upon this product, as well as the human race.

This law in its various changes implies to man the highest creature because of his intellectual capacities, spiritual power, and superior attributes, and just so far as they are exercised will his faculties develop and his soul be benefited. The spirit will benefit itself through the knowledge it is enabled to attain through this form of development.

That the human body had its origin in the lower grades of animals is a fact which we trace beyond the moloch — from the very molecular development. Of this I will not speak now, but may some time be enabled to give you the identical origin of man.

Returning to the Christian spiritual development: The word "Christian" I apply because Christ was the last reformer who diffused so much psychological power to this earth, consisting as it does in magnetic electric forces.

The present generation holds in faith the outgrowth of his works. Believing as they do, that he died for all, they work upon this faith and attract magnetic conditions to harmonize their feelings. In thus doing they are often relieved, if they are sincere, by spiritual attendants, who impart a calm influence, and thus relieve their fears according to their development.

Mortals should now learn to understand that Christ lived to set a noble example to all who can reach with their mind and comprehend with their reason, that his very teachings, which were founded on facts, lay in the atmosphere of the universe.

The tangible facts which he taught lay in the works which he did; the healing of the sick, the curing of the maimed, and the relieving of the oppressed, were traits of his character, the knowledge of which he imparted to his followers, and his very example should be a lasting lesson to all who in their short-sightedness denounce Spiritualism.

He will come again in the clouds were his words. He is even now in the midst of this material atmosphere — not in person, I would not have you believe, but in reflections and expressions, the power of which I have explained to you.

Those very expressions, conveyed in their magnetic descent, will harmonize the magnetic atmosphere ; and mortals developing, striving to reach the fundamental truths of spiritual identity, will attract this magnetism, which unfolds to them the living substances of spiritual knowledge, stimulating the brain through inhalation, and thus assist the spirit to realize the truth.

The errors of dogmatic sects have caused this vast inharmony. The very idea that the blood of one, that the spilling of the blood of one individual can atone for the sins of millions, is sacrilege barbaric, and partakes of the vilest fetishism imaginable. That very idea inspires the soul of man with hauteur and burning vengeance. This we are striving to erase. Host after host of spiritual beings are attracted to earth to revise that fearfully undeveloped idea, which is founded on the grossest errors, and which has in its vile corruption brought suffering and despair to millions of souls.

The dawning, as we term it — the dawning of this beautiful harmonious philosophy which Christ strove so hard to develop in the midst of mortals, brings happy tidings and joyous greetings to many weary mortals. True enough, they receive it according to their development, and apply it according to their comprehension; yet with earnest perseverance, with determined exertion, mortals will be able to outgrow this error, which the dogma of an immaculate conception has impressed on the millions. They will comprehend the fact that salvation lies within themselves. By their own exertions and true merits alone can they save themselves from suffering and remorse.

This planet, earth, being the proper sphere to vegetate the material body — having conditions applicable to the soul and spirit of which I have spoken — it is necessary then to pay strict attention to the growth of the soul, so that the spirit entering upon its new life may have a perfect body. With a perfect body, and general experiences combined with concentrated knowledge, which the mind has acquired through material experiences, the spirit grows in power, and accomplishes noble works in the spirit spheres.

Children, therefore, must be made an object of careful parental watchfulness and guidance. You who are advanced in this knowledge should make rules, the law of which must be positive, for supplying and regulating every condition necessary to their cultivation, compliance with which should be imperative. Spiritually they must be instructed. Let them be taught the chemical laws. Let your Lyceums make scientific experiments in chemical, material, and spiritual magnetism. Let them be made acquainted with this occult force; they must be impressed with every idea of electric power, and the intelligence that can be conveyed to them through it. Give them the highest impressions of moral discipline, and above all impress them with the truth: that they are held accountable for every wrong act committed; that by violating any law of nature, or any law of health, they bring suffering upon themselves; teach them that every moral propensity implanted in their own nature must be strictly watched and guarded with a holy care; that for every law broken through weakness or excessive passion, a penalty is attached, which falls upon themselves, and that they fall to the plane of the animal.

Personal cleanliness is godliness. Godliness so meant is magnetic power which mortals attract to themselves, and which imparts conditions through which the spirit can outgrow material inferiority. By obtaining this power, and adhering to its laws with watchful care, they cultivate will force, which will impart to them everything necessary for their material comfort and spiritual happiness.

COMMUNICATION OF BEN HAMAN.

December 12, 1879.

LOVE and sympathy have again united us this morning. Prompted by the purest of motives, I have come to reveal to you and the masses general knowledge from the spiritual spheres; knowledge by the means of which we hope to benefit humanity, and to assist in their future progress.

Have you the last lecture with you? I want to connect my present lecture with it. I answered "I have not." Then let me collect my thoughts. In a moment or two he began. I will speak of the love and attraction (spoken of in the last chapter) of children toward their parents, who have been drawn from their protecting care and placed under superior matrons.

After they attain their maturity, having every advantage in their spiritual pursuits, attracting strength and power from the positive forces, realized by them in those pursuits, they can and often do impart assistance to their material attractions. They cannot benefit them much until fully matured; then the individuality of their spiritual powers is strengthened by the education which they have acquired in their spiritual training. Experiences of earth add not only to the appreciation of the spiritual, but develop large sympathy for those in the material form.

Arriving at their matured development, they take upon themselves a mission which is pointed out to them by superior guides. That mission is adapted to the spirit, which has acquired particular experiences. If there be need of material experiences, which it may not have fully realized, the pursuit then sought for will be to interblend with the material, and work out upon it effects which prove to be a benefit. If proper conditions are given, the spirit will have opportunities to accomplish its purpose, and strive to remove any obstacle that may be in its way.

If according to the spiritual development the powers assist, then through its intellectual perceptiveness it can realize and see the necessity of sympathy, harmony, and general reform. They strive to accomplish their purposes, not only for the benefit of those to whom they are attracted, but in a liberal way they unfold and impart to all who have a desire to spiritualize their nature. Knowing, as mortals should, the developing power of spiritual sympathy, which develops perpetual harmony, the culture of this power will impart strength to mortals. If they but turn their thoughts in that direction, they can, by the development of their spiritual faculties, produce any effect they desire to accomplish.

In permitting the spirit to control the body when it is educated or developed, as we call it, in the knowledge of this science, they will be enabled to control disease, which destroys so many prematurely, or in the reproductive form which lays such sad stress over the majority of the human race — conception, which is to many a mother a burden laden with sorrow. This can all be controlled through the action of the will upon the uterus. There need be no children born as legal intruders. Unwelcome as such are, the spirit feels the cold formality which is thrown over its body, in fact, formed within the soul.

This should be studied carefully. If there are a less number of children born, and these with more perfect organizations for the spirit of each to develop itself through, the human race will become more perfect, and the incarnated spirit be provided with better conditions for the attainment of its purpose. However, laying aside all prejudices toward their offspring, parents should consider that they have entered on a high mission when they accept that of reproduction.

This act which reproduces the human race, termed sexual intercourse, must be considered holy, and should not be abused. Look at the lower grade of animals; incited by material instinct, male and female alike attain their natural periods. The male never imposing on the female without her proper condition and consent. This I am sorry to say we rarely find in the higher development — that of the human race. Many times offspring are forced upon the female without her consent; she being a slave to the passions of man, conceives from the semen, which conveys in its germs the very embodiment of his own nature. She resents with feelings of contempt and remorse; then the fetal development grows with inharmonious influences preying upon it. In this way children are born into material life with a soul that cannot develop harmony or affection for any mortal.

Fathers and mothers frequently suffer from the vile natures of such offspring; hatred, revenge, and criminal conduct develop themselves in the material growth of such offspring. Let it be understood by the intelligent masses that it is necessary to cultivate the spiritual nature of father and mother before accepting the mission of parentage. Do you wonder at so much misery, so much disobedience, such want of respect for parents shown by their offspring? Who is to blame for this? They themselves. True enough it was in ignorance they produced, but ignorance does not exempt from suffering.

In creating mortals God, the infinite, has given to all alike reasoning powers to be used in compliance with the will, and if they neglect the cultivation of it they must suffer the penalty. This is the sin; by violating the harmonious law of nature, they bring suffering upon themselves; they bruise their own heads and cannot erase the scar until they learn to realize that the harmonious laws of nature are not to be trifled with. Earnest and sincere study must be made in order to comprehend laws which are violated every day by the ignorant masses.

In cultivating the spirit, mind becomes powerful, and the nervous system interblends more with the spiritual than with the material; consequently there cannot be so much added to the material. Nor are there so many children born from parents who have cultivated intellects. The reproductive organs of the material body are absorbed by the spiritual and intellectual. Mind produces more power by cultivation and becomes more productive in spiritual power. Consequently the theory of reproducing from the material to the spiritual builds itself on this fact, that an active mind which plans future objects, designs, will work them out effectually by exerting the will and manipulating effects in the material body.

The spirit of one individual often sees in advance of another. That is owing to the organic development of the material body, and the conditions in which it was conceived.

Napoleon Bonaparte's decisive will, his penetrating perception, and his success in accomplishing his purposes, were all attributable to his organic development.

Spirit guides can impart more benefit and assistance to a perfect organization than to an imperfect one, and if one has more success in the acquirement of material benefit and assistance than another, it is owing to a superior organic development. In every case we trace the advantage which a perfect organization has over an imperfect one. This parents should observe, for they can only blame themselves for the disadvantages and the non-success their children meet in the experience of this earth life.

From Confucius.

December 12, 1879.

Bright hopes now descend upon thee with a power that is divine;
Life and light will e'er attend thee from the spheres of the sublime;
Truer souls than they ne'er entered on a mission in this life,
And we strive here to defend you with the mystic power of life.
Oh, thou father of creation! give thy strength to us in power,
And develop with probation this, thy son, in spirit power.

HOW beautiful is life! with all its varying changes! I know that thou hast struggled hard, dear brother, with the cares which often cause sorrow within thy heart. Bear in mind that this is all necessary. The all wise and loving Father has given us strength and power to help thee now, to lift the burdens of care from thy placid brow, and draw thee in closer union with ourselves.

Heretofore life was a mystery to thee; but now, through the fostering care of a loving father, who has revealed to thee the true nature and the natural causes, with their effects in this life, the mystery is disappearing.

Oh, dear brother, realize that my visit to thee is founded upon the affections of a true spiritual love, which germinated thousands of years ago on this earth. Even as thy material body has vegetated through material surroundings, so my spiritual soul germinates in the spiritual spheres, to work out spiritual effects upon thee. Go forth wheree'er thou wilt, reflections ever attend thee, with love and union here instilled; may blessings ever surround thee! . . . My blessing reaches thee from distant spheres. . . .

SKYWAUKE, — Big chief S—— (my father-in-law) come, he say you no keep him promise cause you no bring your squaw here. A — chief (brother-in-law) needs help, wants to draw magnetism. Chief S—— better now, wants to keep young chief. Little squaw here. "My sister?" yes — she happy much power. Mother squaw brings big bunch of flowers to you for Christmas present. Can't ship them over. — (A good test inasmuch as mother was passionately fond of flowers.)

December 19, 1879.

The first part of the communication of November 14 not being clear to me, after the medium was in trance, I asked for a clearer statement of the first four or five sentences, when Ben Haman replied, —

"Mind requires material aid to assist in its development. This condition is imparted to the essence, by the material body which it inhabits. Mind is spirit and requires the material elements of the physical body for its unfoldment. I have told you that the soul and spirit interblend. The soul is the assisting power by which the spirit is sustained, nor could the spirit have material experiences without the assistance of those magnetic elements.

"The magnetic-electric forces combined constitute the soul principle of the material body. The spirit is sustained and assisted by those elements which constitute the soul. The soul is a part of those elements. The soul develops out of the material body, and the body being impregnated with those gases, imparts to the soul the substances by which it attains its growth."

Communication from Confucius.

December 19, 1879.

KIND and noble brother, I greet you with happiness to-day. Your exertions are not in vain. That which you are striving for you will attain. Your Monday *séances*, conducted as they are in harmony and love, assisted by the friends in spirit spheres who are deeply interested in you, add largely to your spiritual development. Your deep faith, sustained by confidence, holds the power, closely united with yourself and the few friends in harmony with you.

The persistency and growth of spiritual affections add largely in attracting the true, the pure, the virtuous souls from the inner spheres of the blessed.

You realized this on last Monday night, when the noble Nazarene, with his pure, magnetic power, imparted to you and your friends the healing balm, and gave you the peace of mind and power to heal the sick and strengthen the weak. Yes, noble brother, your efforts are not in vain. Time alone unfolds this power. Time alone will make conditions through and by which you are assisted; through which the ingrowth of the spiritual unit (link) which holds soul and spirit in close communion with ourselves will be completed.

Perseverance accomplishes purposes. Purposes attain power from the spiritual, through which good effects are interwoven with spiritual designs that are pure and confiding.

"Verily, I say unto you, unless you become as a little child, you cannot enter the kingdom of heaven." Those parables are not correctly defined by the learned souls of that latter day. A man in his material growth, with varying experiences and preconceived ideas, imagines himself self-sustaining. But mortals must learn to comprehend, no matter how old in material years, or how well informed in material experiences, that they are often misguided by error. They must place themselves in a humble condition, and make themselves receptive to the higher and more harmonious laws, through which spiritual knowledge is imparted to man humble and simple in notion and mind. Mortals must bow in obedience to the positive law, through which they attain this knowledge. Wisdom interblends and constitutes a potency through which the will is developed, and this can only be obtained through the perseverance of your individual desires. As you hold the sceptre within your grasp, hold it with firmness and with a decisive desire to work out the noble effects which the Christian mind strives for — truth, firmness, and implicit confidence in the great Creator. Through confidence alone can you attract this power. Faith and will will come to your assistance. The trio interblend as one and constitute the spiritual will.

Yes, noble brother, through perseverance and a desire to do good with confidence and love you have drawn the Nazarene hither, who interests himself as much now as he did in his travail while on earth. Even more and greater is the power which emits its effulgent rays to illume the pathway of struggling souls who seek to find the spiritual path, in which they will be guided to a higher and happier life.

Persevere and do not become weary. Hold your will firm, and all you desire will be realized. Farewell, and be happy.

COMMUNICATION FROM BEN HAMAN.

January 2, 1880.

MORTALS should be particularly instructed what course to pursue and how to live a more perfect life. The spiritual body is developed out of the soul. The soul growth develops out of the material body, consequently the soul partakes of material substances, for without them it could not develop. The grosser the food the coarser the development, and it should be understood that natures endowed with a high degree of knowledge can and do develop a high spiritual power.

As before stated, gross material, let it be in substance of any kind, will injure the spiritual sense, making it weak in its perceptions. Those who live simply upon vegetables and fruit develop the perceptive power and are very impressive. The physical body must be properly cared for. If you desire to develop the spiritual nature, you must obey this law, for by its observance, which is so essential to present as well as future happiness, much suffering and disease will be avoided.

Alas! the weak, debilitated nature demands with craving appetite the grosser! By the majority this depraved appetite is gratified.

We desire to call your attention to this law. Purity within can only be developed by the practice of external purity. Regular habits in the mode of living are essential. When the physical body is cared for, the spiritual nature of the individual interblends with the purer elements, and is assisted by the more developed spiritual powers. You will often observe in debilitated persons those who are very sensitive to external surroundings, the appetite failing; they partake of very little gross food, nourishing on very simple diets. Such persons become very sensitive to visions and impressions. All mediums are more or less of this character, nor are they ever entirely restored to a robust physical state of health. They must be relieved of pain, which can be drawn from them by magnetic manipulations of their spiritual guides in attendance; but the more sensitive the physical body becomes the more ethereal it becomes in its perceptions. You will find that most of the mortals who are sensitive in their natures are delicate in their organizations.

All more or less could develop this power if they gave their attention to it. Over two-thirds of the human race might become independent mediums by giving attention to the laws of nature. All are endowed with mediumistic power; but, as before stated, it is destroyed by a gross manner of living.

To observe, as we do, the present inharmonious nature which mortals encourage and develop, would make you despair of ever accomplishing much good; but we view it from a different standpoint; we who are workers in this great harmonial philosophy never become weary. The persistent energy of our will interblends with the magnetism of mortals with such positive force that it must make an impression; if not at first, it will at last.

This power is well understood by all scientific minds, but they do not apply it to the right purpose. We may get weary at times when the individual will of those whom we desire to influence is too positive, when it holds itself askance, influenced or attracted to the material, giving vent to passions, and giving themselves up to angry demonstrations. When such is the case, the pure, sensitive spirit withdraws for the time being, and the more undeveloped press forward and hold high carnival with the power they are permitted to display. Angry passions should be suppressed; they are more injurious to the spiritual nature than all else combined. They are not only composed of the incensed passions of the mind, but impregnated with a low order of spiritual force, and often under the impulse of the moment mortals are given to crime, the dark stain of which cannot be erased. When such is the case they place themselves under heavy responsibility to the injured individual. This nature is generally developed in the physical organs of the individual, and can very easily be modified by spiritual magnetism which is imparted at every *séance*. If mortals sit in harmony and sincerity those evil defects can be removed, and the good, harmonious powers will interblend and give strength and happiness.

This philosophy is the true religion, if you wish to call it such, of nature. It has always existed, and in the remotest days exerted greater power upon the human family than now. Through misconceived ideas which mortals themselves form, through the passions and selfish motives it has been undermined, and the influences drawn hither could not impart their intellectual power to mortals, for they in their positive spirit designed and worked out the effects according to their views.

This is why you have such a variety of sects. Each nation, according to its intellectual capacities, has formed its own God, and made its own heaven. Error is at the root of all evil, and not until this can be eradicated, and the true philosophy established in its place, will there be harmony and peace among earth's children.

There are many ways by which spiritual truth is imparted and made known to the children of earth. The greatest of all is the electric inventions, concerning which truths are imparted with double force to students who seek to acquaint themselves with this elementary power.

Spiritual light imparts strength and vitality to the physical body of man, and gives power and strength to the spirit. It is the life fluid upon which the spirit subsists while in the material body, and through its demonstrative power it acts upon the material sense of mortals, convincing them of the greater power beyond. Even the most undeveloped minds would stand aghast at the explosive power of this electric force. Your simple batteries which are used for electrifying the nervous system, are proofs of the positive life force existing in this element. It is only through scientific development in nature's demonstrative laws that the human race will eventually harmonize and grow more spiritual.

The earth is gradually passing through a change, perfecting itself and developing a purer atmosphere. Those obnoxious gases which are being thrown off constantly are being consumed by the electric positive force; and as this purification proceeds the purer life forces will have more power to impregnate with greater force, or strengthen the individual body as well as vegetable matter. Gradually this vapor becomes less, and the elements surrounding your atmosphere become purer, and the electric forces are not weakened by the poisonous gases emanating from the soil.

This law, when rightly understood, will largely aid in developing the spiritual sense of man, for man or mortals cannot see, as many of them claim, a body develop out of nothing. The spirit body is composed of physical organized electricity. These substances, it is true, are not perceptible to the eye in a negative state, but when acted upon by positive force are perceptible; for instance, when the elements are inharmonious. This results from an excessive power of the vapory substances which arise from the earth and penetrate the atmosphere. Coming in contact with oxygen and hydrogen they innoculate the electricity, which is the purest force and the most positive, and immediately destroy the negative — consume it. This is what you call the lightning flashes, which the eye can see flashing through the atmosphere in a thunder storm. This will cease, but many thousands of years hence, when the earth's soil will have developed out of this crude state. Vapors will never cease; moisture is essential to animal and vegetable life, but they will become purer, the air will not be innoculated with those poisonous gases which are so destructive to human and animal life. Throwing these off incessantly, as the earth is now doing, they will eventually be consumed by the creative force, which is electricity. This force, so purifying in its process, creates other planets out of the very substances thrown off in a more refined form and drawn from this and other planets.

COMMUNICATION OF BEN HAMAN.

January 9, 1880.

THERE is nothing lost in material. Substances not perceptible to the eye interblend with other forces, and are used to produce material objects. The chemical analysis of different substances which men have made a study proves this. It is a demonstrated fact, not only in spiritual sciences, but in material observations, that the magnetism thrown off from the sun, which illuminates this earth, contains this creative power largely developed, the force of which is perceptible in the development of animal and vegetable life in the material. You find that plants perish without the sun's rays; they wither, fade, and die. Human life also depends upon the electric-magnetic rays of the sun. If mortals would but use their faculties to think, they would convince themselves of this law of nature. But the great majority (weak and ignorant creatures) allow others to do their thinking for them; they do not use or exercise their faculties any more than if they did not possess them. How can any spiritual identity be developed in such material bodies? None can think for you. You must acquire your own individuality by exerting your faculties and striving to comprehend. That the sun possesses creative power is a positive fact demonstrable to all scientific minds, or minds endowed with a comprehensive knowledge.

All matured planets follow in direct rotary motion round the central force of a sun. Those magnetic rays draw them in their orbitary rotation, and some of them have been entirely consumed. When drawn within the rotary current of the positive which consumes, what becomes of the entire mass? It is transferred or conveyed to other planets which are in direct rotation, and assists in their development or construction.

The magnetic power of the sun's rays throws off a great deal of substance in a gaseous form, which comes in contact with other electric-magnetic substances of the atmosphere, from which other planets develop themselves.

In the first formation of a planet it is a vapory or gaseous substance, composed of these concentrated forces. It gradually expands in dimensions. As additional atoms are attracted to it, it becomes a luminous body, drifting hither and thither until sufficient positive elements are attained; then it becomes more solid, and attracts, like a magnet, more solid substances thrown off from planets already matured. Those solid substances are consumed immediately by the electric force, and aid in developing a yet more solid material. In this way the planet on which you live was made. The forces of nature are both positive and negative. The positive electric force cannot create without the negative magnetic force. The two are as essential to each other as the light of day is to distinguish the darkness of night.

Life has indeed been a mystery to men. They know not whence it comes nor whither it goes, and yet they know they live. Is it not then a duty to learn to comprehend why you live, and what you live for, not simply vegetate and die as an animal or as a plant? Mortals must learn to realize that they are not mere animals, to live merely to gratify their sensual appetites and then perish; but that they are spiritual beings, possessing a life that is indestructible, that is above everything existing on this planet, the immortal soul or spirit.

Therefore, attention must be given in this direction. Men must learn to comprehend that it lies within their power to cultivate the spirit and soul; that for this purpose they live in the material body. Now, with this positive knowledge, they begin to recognize the hidden germ which lies within the material body.

Efforts are now made by spiritual guides who are endowed with power, through the changing conditions of nature's laws, to approach earth's children. They come in bodies, in large circles, to assist in the development of spiritual power. True, the elementary forces are still doing their work, as they have been for millions of years, but not with the same results. For, through the changing laws or atmospheric conditions before spoken of, they are losing power; but much depends on yourselves in developing out of their power.

Mortals must turn their attention to the purer, to the harmonial and sincere spiritual, and put confidence and faith in their immortal disembodied friends, for they possess power to assist them. "Let there be light, and there was light." Faith, confidence, and sincerity will assist mortals, all of whom fully realize that they must pass away, in developing this spiritual knowledge. Everything that lives in the flesh or has a material origin is perishable. The pressure of the electric forces eventually consumes everything material.

Therefore mortals must learn to realize that it is vain folly to lay up stores for their material glory. It is only by doing good to one another that they can lay up rich stores for material fame and spiritual glory. Doing good to one another, forgetful of self-aggrandizement, doing it as a labor of love, and a spiritual glory follows. They who strive to assist each other will find when they enter spirit life that they have many times helped a dear and near one in spirit, many times an own spirit offspring, sister or brother, possibly a father or mother.

"Ye know not whence ye come nor whither ye go," but let the spirit of truth abide with you forever. As the spirit develops and outgrows the material desires, it becomes more sympathetic, more harmonious, and more Godlike. The highly cultivated and intellectual are more charitable and more sympathetic with their fellow-beings. They see through a clearer light and comprehend through a purer sense. Through progression they learn to realize that they too, in one period of life, stood on the lower planes of material experiences, and that through repeated changes with advantages in spirit they were drawn higher. Exertion of the faculties, with power of will, will assist largely in outgrowing material conditions.

What have they who give themselves up to material pleasures, gratifying the material cravings of the physical body, and feeding themselves with all the grosser substances, gained? Nothing but disadvantages deleterious to the spirit and soul. Failure after failure of the spirit is produced in this wise.

The ecclesiastics of various denominations give themselves up to this destructive power, which is a weakness of the flesh. Their education consists in memorizing purely theological dogmas, which pertain entirely to the material. Consequently nothing spiritual can develop out of it. Their God or Deity is a material being, endowed with passions of various characters, inciting to wrath and punishment. Do not wonder that they themselves in their researches are weak in faith! They have no staff upon which they can lean; their faith is of a material origin and must perish.

We find many sceptics, many atheists, among the clergy. "Let us live well while we do live. We know not what the morrow may bring," is the motto of many. They have searched the Scriptural philosophy, have acquired a historic knowledge of traditions, and they find very little comfort in a perusal of the lives of undeveloped nations, — nations springing up in fungal growth and perishing in the rays of the sun. They cannot be teachers. Such men are as weak as the infant in your arms. It is simply ridiculous to build hopes and trust your future to the spiritual assistance of such; they hold no power within their atmosphere.

Teachers by whom the spiritual philosophy is advocated and diffused must be pure themselves, pure and sincere. A sceptic can make no impression. There must be that inner conviction which knowledge alone imparts, to make an impression with intensified power. This inner conviction which strengthens the soul is a positive force, originating with the supreme Creator.

This is the fountain of life, and can be attained by every individualized soul who strives to comprehend. And this is life. Knowledge is life; combined with power it gives force to the will, which, when acting upon the positive forces of nature, can create objects.

Thousands upon thousands lead a mere vegetable or animal life. They cultivate no soul; they perish with the animal. This does not mean that they do not live after death, but in what state or form (?) is well known to us. They merely exist, the elements imparting conditions by which they sustain themselves. They return not endowed with power to develop or progress, but simply to live in a state of apathy, constantly fearing everything which approaches. It is a dread, a fear, an agony over which they have no control, either to throw off or develop out of. And in thus moving hither and thither, they are caught within the current of revolving force, many times consumed and destroyed, and then again brought in contact with the material conditions of this planet, and are assisted to reincarnate, which is an assistance to them. The next lecture will explain why mortals cling with such tenacity to life.

Communication from Ben Haman.

January, 16, 1880.

GOD bless you, my son! The bright sun rays shower down their atoms, giving life to the vegetable and animal kingdom.

INVOCATION. — O nature! in thy bountiful unfoldment we trace in every object the love of the great Creator. As the attributes of all that is good, all that is pure, emanate from thy divine power, we ask a blessing upon these loved ones before us. May they be strengthened by the rays of this magnetic orb, and guided through life by thy most supreme love. May the attributes of thy will unfold their natures with charity toward earth's children. May they feel, through thy positive will, that the development of their patience must unfold to suffering humanity, with assistance from the spiritual spheres. O Father and Mother God! may the attributes of thy omnipotent will inspire their souls with love, truth, and knowledge, linking them closer to the great affinitized power, through which they will be enabled to work out thy infinite purposes. Father of love and truth, give us power through thy emanative love to guide their footsteps in the path of duty; and may they ever feel through our guiding care and our administrative love, that they are led higher and higher in spiritual aspirations. May they feel that by overcoming the material cares and burdens imposed upon them, they are gaining victory over death and sin. This we ask of thee, O Father and Mother, thou dual of all that is good, of all that is holy. Amen.

"Have you the book with you," asked Ben Haman. "Yes," I answered. "Please read the last sentence, so that I may connect this communication with the last one. I said, " I have no spectacles with me, and cannot read." — "Then give me the book." I happened to hand it upside down to the medium, who, in a deep trance, with eyes closed, took the book, turned over some forty pages, until she reached the end of the last communication in manuscript. After holding it before her face some minutes, it being still upside down, her eyes all the time closed, she dictated the following: —

WHY MORTALS CLING WITH TENACITY TO LIFE.

Life consists or coexists in all things; all things contain life. There are three distinct forms of life. There is the essence divine, the outgrowth of all material substances, which is spirit, so called, and indestructible. Then the material which exhibits in its development the animeline substance which constitutes growth and has its inflation from the same source. Then the material substances composed from the material soil, inflated with the same material of life, varying only in material substances, such as the mineral, vegetable, and animal kingdoms. The same positive electric forces, combined with the negative creative forces, inflate every living substance on this orb.

Humanity has outgrown the lower order of development, through incessant repetition, and stands the highest and first of all material life. Developing through spiritual aspirations, the intellectual power of the will or mind, it interblends with the higher creative power, and with repeated experiences has progressed beyond all other life.

This power so often spoken of, yet so imperfectly understood by mortals, is the creative power of life, and the constituted developer of form. These solar rays of the sun, which penetrate the soil, impregnating it with living germs, thrown off from the various planets, and conveyed to this planet, impregnates the soil, developing mineral and vegetable life. Without these solar rays there no life could exist. The very atmosphere which surrounds you has living germs developed through the effulgent rays of this solar power. Imbuing the material organs with strength, it also impregnates the blood of the human system, inhaled, as before stated, through respiration, not only by the lungs, but by the molecules of the whole physical body externally.

Life is developed within the germ of everything which has an organic development: consequently, all things have an organic development, even the seed. As the seed develops and matures within the soil from the penetrative rays of the sun, so the acorn, with its tiny unfoldment, matures for reproducing the oak-tree. But why do they require darkness for their first development? Simply because the positive rays of the sun would destroy or consume the life principle developed in the germ. Both positive and negative are essential in the unfoldment and development of life. The positive alone is destructive without the negative. The acorn, in its matured germ, consists in or contains the fullest power of the positive force. It requires to be placed within the soil, where it is not exposed to the positive electric rays, but receives a full portion through the diffusion of the power in the soil. The soil is the reproductive negative matter; it contains various chemical properties, according to its kind, and imparts the necessary conditions to the acorn, expanding the germ in the negative surroundings. But the rays of this electric power penetrate, as you see, in a milder form the soil, and give it (the acorn) the vigor which sends it upward out of its immured position for more perfect development by this electric force. Invigorated by both electric and magnetic rays combined, it is drawn higher and higher. The soil imparting more of the chemical magnetic conditions to the root, strengthening fibre after fibre, shooting up in its current to the very trunk, giving strength and vigor to its growth. The electric rays of the sun impart the more positive power, through which it becomes hardened and withstands the pressure of the elements and the rage of the storm.

This is the vegetable life, requiring, as it does, the electric power for its development. When dead, it returns to both the electric and negative. One portion, the foliage and the sap as you call it, the sap from which the foliage is produced, returns to the positive or electric. It is drawn out by the positive rays and diffused again among the elements. The trunk decays, replenishing the soil with the negative matter, whose particles through intermixing produce the same, varying very little in change of matter from that in which the acorn was first developed.

And so life repeats itself in every form of the vegetable kingdom, varying very little in quality or kind. Only when man, with his intellectual capacities, studies the biography of this law, i.e., the physiology of vegetation, is he enabled to change and perfect the quality of vegetable growth by applying external conditions which are assisted by the electric forces. Only the negative forces will always impart the same conditions when repeated in the same soil; but the electric pressure will perfect everything, if you study the law and learn how to apply it.

The development of life requires darkness, and through a proper study of this science you will observe that it goes back to the remotest germ of mineral unfoldment. If the seed planted in the soil requires darkness to develop it, so with the higher forms of life; animal and human also require darkness out of which they too are developed.

The human form is developed out of the animal kingdom. It is a higher form of soul growth, and yet depends upon the same conditions. Nature with its creative power imparts to one and all alike in this particular law of production.

The fish in the ocean will lay its ova in a secluded spot, where, through instinct acquired by its own development, it knows the exact and proper conditions necessary. True, there are amphibians that place their ova within the solar rays, such as the serpent and the turtle and various other reptiles. But mind you the living germ is incased within a shell, which gives the proper magnetic protection from the more positive element.

So with the human germ, an outline of which I have already given you in this work — that of conception. The ova, being impregnated with the semen, is drawn within the womb and develops there. Darkness alone imparts the negative condition. Consequently the magnetic part of a mortal is the soul, which can develop only in darkness the life-germ of a material character.

It is only after the infant is born, expelled from its dark vault, thrown within the positive electric rays of this solar power, that it receives the positive spirit which imbues the whole system with an invigorated power, and sound or voice is developed immediately from the current power of this life force.

Why is it, then, that mortals cling with tenacity to life? Simply this: the whole material body, being composed of every substance existing in the mineral and vegetable kingdom, it holds its attraction in assimilation toward its origination, or toward that from out of which it developed children of nature. The spirit intellectually unfolds itself according to the organic construction of the physical body.

Yet the spirit may have had, and has had, experiences in the spiritual spheres, which often leave a bad impression, in the way of fear, which preys upon the thought, and in returning to the material body it makes an impression on the sensorium, or organ of life, and follows it in its experiences through the material life; and if not lifted, through development and progression, above this sphere or plane, it continues in this state of fear until it separates from the body, that is called the fear of death, being ignorant of all that follows after the material life, and especially, if the spirit has had hard experiences in former lives, it cannot partake of anything good, but is harassed by reflections of the past, which impregnates the fear of coming in contact with that which may be the same in effect as was the past.

But through knowledge which is self-aspiration and a power the immortal spirit is assisted through the more positive guides to comprehend that they can overpower all evil, and attain through the all-aspiring will a position of independence by which the soul is strengthened; for, when it attains individuality, the spirit feeds the soul with positive force. Conviction after conviction follows through this development. The independent spirit cares nothing more for the material and its perishable effects, but strives to attain its individuality through the positive assistance, which you all can attract by exerting the will power in attaining knowledge for your development.

And thus mortals overcome the fear of death only by striving to acquire knowledge and acquainting themselves with the higher laws of magnetism, which convey a substance for the soul growth and a power to assist the spiritual unfoldment; only through self-exertion can they convince themselves that the change of death is but an aspiration to a higher life.

If the spirit is not fully matured to realize this change for the higher and more elevated development of an existent futurity, it will repeat itself, to vegetate upon the very soil and in the very atmosphere to which it clings with such tenacity, and from which it can only be separated by the progressive law of individuality.

All experiences are necessary to bring the spirit upon this elevated position. Good and evil, sorrow and suffering — all are produced by one great infinite soul principle. And evil is as essential as the good, for if there were no sorrow, there could be no joy : it is only by experiencing the deepest sorrow that joy can be appreciated. If you were never separated from your friends or loved companion, you would not know the grief that separation causes, nor could you realize the happiness and joy a reunion imparts.[1]

---

[1] Unless pain follows discord, joy cannot follow concord. — *Tho'ts from a Giver of Tho'ts.*

And so we trace the evil and interblend it with the good, for if there were not this dual, separated as it is, there would not be an established whole of a united and permanent power.

Communication from Ben Haman.

January 26, 1880.

MUCH depends upon the soul of the medium through whom we converse. If an operator has a musical instrument highly strung, in accord with harmony and sound, he can produce perfect music. So with us. This medium is the instrument. Her spirit is not used by us; the soul remains in her body, but the thought or spirit withdraws, is thrown out. We control the instrument with the remaining life or soul, as you perceive. Our positive magnetism overcasts her whole body. And with psychological force we impress the words in language on her sensorium.

Now, if the instrument is imbued with all material propensities, if the soul's desire is merely for gross material, and partakes of them freely, the finer forces cannot make an impression; for the whole body is subtile to the influence imparted to it, and we cannot produce that which we could if the medium were developed into a more spiritual condition. So does trouble or sorrow of any kind make an impression upon the organs of life or brain.

We find in this medium traits of character, developments which incline purely to the spiritual. Could she be withdrawn from material cares, over which she worries greatly, causing a constant pressure on her spirit; could she be lifted above these, her development would be of the highest order. And there is no telling of the immeasurable truths which could be given through her; all consists in development.

You have hundreds and hundreds of mediums, entirely upon a material plane. Few comprehend the law of development. Truly it consists in more than making simple material conditions. The soul and spirit must develop into the sciences of nature. The psychic force assists them largely. All mediums who wish to be true workers in this cause must acquit themselves with the laws of psychology, through which the philosophy develops itself, through the comprehension of interior and external force. Unless the medium acquires knowledge from this source, assisted by the will power of his own intuitive nature, he cannot benefit others. A medium must be pure and unprejudiced, in order to impart pure magnetism to others. This evil will be remedied after awhile. Gradually the negatives are drawn within the circle of spiritual sympathy, and they will learn from observation that it is to their advantage to develop a pure soul, through the teaching of moral discipline. Physiologists dare not reveal the truth, although they comprehend it. Selfish motives prompt them to keep it to themselves, lest humanity become too wise, and their practice be cut short. The teaching of moral discipline would cause a prevalence of knowledge in all who have intelligence to comprehend, and the spread of diseases be stopped, if not destroyed. Theologians who profess to be teachers of divinity, should not hesitate to speak of those ills which flesh is heir to, and should demonstrate against them. They, too, are dormant, many times owing to their ignorance, but more often to their own sensual nature.

However, the world moves, and the human race is moving on with it. Eventually in the tide of time a more moral school will be established. Human nature is striving for something above the material. The inclination of those who give themselves the opportunity to think is drawn from the gross material, and feels the disappointment — a vacuum that cannot impart happiness. All, all will follow in one and the same rotation, and eventually in the progress of time, the purer souls will emerge out of the darkness into the light of spiritual purity.

There may be harmony between you and the medium, but there cannot always be harmony between the spirit and the control of the medium. If the control is not developed up to our sphere, we cannot establish that link which is necessary to impart the thought, by which knowledge is conveyed.

Here is an organism, here is a spirit in the body, pure and sensitive in a high degree. She exhausts herself, sacrifices herself for the advancement of others. The perceptions of those standing on a lower plane cannot reach to a comprehension of those who stand upon a higher one, and they who are undeveloped have no charity for their fellow-mortals. The undeveloped are as poisonous to the developed as the sting of the adder is to the flesh, and the most sensitive are the first to succumb to the poison.

COMMUNICATION FROM H. S.

February 2, 1880.

FATHER H. S. — Ed, I come to give you my blessing. Ed, there are many things to learn in the spirit world — things I had not thought of while on earth, which had I have known I might have avoided much suffering and helped you all. I am happy now, made happy through your mother's noble exertions and experiences. Her spiritual soul was developed while in the body, and in spiritual life has made my soul happy. I was always happy when I was in the material. I did not develop much spirituality, simply because I was happy in my home. Had I met some great sorrow, I might have turned my attention to spiritual things. I have not suffered any torments. I might have done more to spiritualize my children. Ed : you have made conditions. Through your perseverance you attract spiritual beings from a very high plane. While one communicates through the organs of this lady, others are giving instructions. We are inspired by superior beings, who inform us what course to pursue to elevate ourselves. This philosophy is not founded on faith, but on works which are actual and real : and they who come over leaning on faith alone for happiness or salvation will be terribly disappointed.

I find this spiritual world as active, as real, as the one I lived in with yourself. The only thing which seemed a little strange at first was that I could not approach my children. I could approach your mother nearer than I could approach you. She seemed to know intuitively what I wanted. Through this power I led her to investigate Spiritualism. I found it was the only true way by which I could expect to help her or my children.

Ed : we are drawn intuitively to those we love. We have no power to control this feeling. It seems to emanate from the soul, to those we love in the material, regardless of the will. You have done us great good. If Rush and Fanny could be brought within the knowledge, how much happier they would be and able to do so much more good to others!

You attract many whom I did not know. Spirit bodies strengthen themselves by the spiritual magnetism you attract here. If you had never made these conditions, I never would have been enabled to say I was self-sustaining, and enabled to do some good to others. This seems to be the law of progression.

Mother sends her love and blessing. Frank and Will send their love. Henry sends his gratitude and best wishes.

COMMUNICATION FROM BEN HAMAN.

February 2, 1880.

GROSS food is essential in some cases. It depends largely upon the physical development of the body. There are some bodies so constituted that they require gross food, and are benefited largely by the moderate use of it. It should be taken with sanitary conditions, never in large quantities, always with a vegetable diet in assistance, to which the interblending propensities impart to the body the proper essences through and by which the body is developed.

True, in the spiritual development of mortals very little gross food is required, for, as the spirit progresses, the body develops into the spiritual power which sustains it, through the magnetism imparted by the spiritual beings which surround it. This magnetism is nutritious to the material body, and less food is required by those who are spiritual in nature than by those who are more material. As mortals progress out of this material life, the more will they adapt themselves to a vegetable and fruit diet; for by thus applying their mental attractions to the more spiritual powers, the less will be the desire for gross, sensual things which hold mortals chained, as it were, to the earth sphere.

These very *séances*, when conducted on a high plane, with sincerity and confidence by both the medium and sitters, are very beneficial to both the physical body and the spiritual development. The magnetism imparted to them from the spiritual band unfolds the organs of the body, impregnating the soul with those pure elements, and thus develops the spirit into a conscious desire for the pure, the moral, and the virtuous.

We encourage more *séances*, but they should always be conducted with the purest spiritual motives. The moral development of the human race must come from this source. Spiritual natures, or mortals endowed with the desire to unfold the spiritual nature, will readily realize and apply the pure knowledge which is imparted to them, through which they become individualized, or their individuality becomes perceptible to themselves by the self-sustaining power which is imparted to them, through the effort they make in seeking for the higher perceptions of immortality. Life, indeed, would be nothing to man or woman if it were all material, if they had nothing to hope for in futurity. It is the absolute knowledge which convinces the immortal soul of a future existence. Knowledge conveys clear ideas, develops intellectual perceptions, through which faculty after faculty develops itself, and the mind becomes convinced of a superior force existing in nature's laws, which imparts the all-convincing power of this indestructible matter.

Through searching with a desire to penetrate the heretofore incomprehensible ethers which constitute so much activity in a tangible form, immortal souls are drawn into the spiritual atmosphere, where a knowledge is imparted to the perceptive mind, imparting to it a self-sustaining entity, the strength of which gives a power to the spirit, through which the spirit is made self-sustaining.

That which mortal eye has seen in a tangible form it does not doubt; that which the material hands have grasped of solid substances, the senses cannot question the existence of. So with the spiritual sense of mortals: that which it has penetrated the knowledge of which gives the full assurance of an identity which really exists in a tangible form to the spiritual sense, can never be doubted; for an impression once made by this ethereal power cannot be otherwise than enduring, for it imparts a strength to the perceptive power of the soul that makes it self-sustaining, and there is no material power on earth that can ever destroy it; for in substance it supersedes everything which is of a material origin.

Consequently we say, "Knowledge is power," and power is a force through and by which material objects are controlled and spiritual reproduction developed.

I wish to concentrate the work. The one I will give you will supersede that which I have given before, if the material conditions of the medium are successfully arranged. She is more flexible than when I began. She is developing — her perceptive organs are developing. If she would keep herself to a few controls, we could more readily impart knowledge. Sir Albrecht (her guide) desires a very few to control her.

A medium is not acting on her own individuality half the time (I speak of the trance); she is retarded by being controlled by the undeveloped. Remember me to the medium with my best wishes.

Communication from Ben Haman.

February 9, 1880.

AGAIN we meet to express our thoughts — thoughts from the invisible to the visible. What a vast difference there is between those who do and those who do not comprehend this beautiful philosophy! They who live simply for the material; they who give their minds to material things, cannot realize that it is possible that spiritual beings can have power to communicate with earth's children.

How much happier they would be if they could comprehend that friends in spirit form are as tangible to their external senses as mortals are in the material form.

The great Infinite principle created in ourselves and in all finite creatures, the spiritual-essence, is the God principle in mortals; and if they would strive to know more of themselves, to comprehend the individuality of their own nature, how much better it would be for each and every one of them!

It certainly would lighten the burdens of this life; it would show them in a clearer light that mortals can and do make their own conditions for happiness or misery. Would that they could but realize with perfect confidence that *there is a future life!*

Too little attention is paid to the cultivation of the spirit. Mortals in their material course neglect their physical bodies, and thereby impoverish the soul, and weaken the spiritual faculties. By learning and observing the true conditions necessary for the unfoldment of the soul, the spirit realizes with true perceptive ability every condition necessary for its development.

Yes, mortals can and do make their heaven, and make their hell, so to speak. Is it not to every soul's advantage and benefit to make himself or herself happy? Then why grope along in this way; hither and thither, crushed with despondency and overburdened with cares, when it is so easy to reach for the higher and purer development, which can be imparted to every individual if they desire it.

According to the unfoldment of the inner nature each and every individual receives and comprehends. Knowledge is applied according to the development of the spiritual faculties. Mortals conceive as they comprehend it, or as they have been taught in youth. Education forming character, as you know, it stands to reason that they cannot realize anything superior to that which their faculties led them to believe. Knowledge of spiritual things gives strength to the faculties, and enables the perceptive power to unfold itself with more strength and a higher conception of the internal possibilities of the spirit. Consequently we must strive to develop more spiritual teachers. When we say develop, we apply the verb, in impressible individuals, persons so organized that we can reach them with our influence by impressions or otherwise; sensitive beings, who will give their time and attention to spiritual pursuits, through which they will be drawn higher into the atmosphere of angels, who will be able to impart to them power and strength to instruct earth's children.

However, to educate or develop beings, surrounded as they are with all the undeveloped conditions which this material sphere imparts, requires time. It requires much power, much strength, on our side, to protect them from those conditions. This we wish to instil into the minds of those acquainted with this philosophy, those who have been largely benefited through the angel visits of their friends, those who have been led higher into the spheres of wisdom, those whose minds have been expanded by intellectual truths, so that they will be enabled to remove the shackles from the slave-bound souls of materialism, that they may be enabled to liberate themselves, to break the chains of sectarianism, and remove the prejudice which binds the whole to one form of infidelity.

Yes, my friends, it must and will come. The light which evolves in the surrounding atmosphere of this planet, the reflections of which are thrown over all alike; this light which has its birth in the intellectual spheres, is imparted as a soothing balm to the creed-bound souls of avaricious orthodoxy, the faith in which so many place their trust and confidence, only to be disappointed again and again when they enter the higher life.

To these favored ones, who have power to comprehend the divine philosophy of nature's laws, they who are fathers and mothers, we send a voice, an appeal for assistance. As you cherish your future happiness, O parents of souls intrusted to your care, as you appreciate their welfare as you should as well as your own, instruct them in this truth!

Take truth for the motto of your labors here; work it out with effectiveness toward those souls, those finite beings placed under your fostering care; teach them the true philosophy of nature; let their minds be brought up in the true light of the divine laws which control all things, free from creeds and forms and sects of every kind.

When the young mind is instructed by objects which are with unreserved confidence placed before it, with careful observation and study, it grows stronger and firmer in the spiritual unfoldment, grasping ideas, thoughts, and objects with explicit force, the assurance of which gives double strength to the soul and force to the will, which, when directed to mortals inferior, must act like an electric fluid upon the vapory atmosphere, and make an impression upon them; for only superior intellect can control inferior.

It is absolutely essential that mortals give their attention in this direction.

That ignorance develops suffering is a vied fact, which is proven to every individual if they will carefully investigate it. Ignorance is sin, for all suffering imparts to the individual a sense of anguish, from which there is no power of escape, unless they discover means through which they can relieve themselves.

Any crime committed, or any wrong done to your brother, will strike the cerebral nerve of your physical body and cause you to feel nervous and depressed. How will you be able to erase this? Simply by establishing harmony between you and the injured party by confessing your wrong, and his acknowledgment of your sincerity, the ray of light will reflect on your soul and give you peace. The harmony again established gives the spirit guides conditions to remove or erase the suffering, which is remorse.

O brother man! brothers of one great and vast principle, would to God I had the power to convince you of the necessity for you to strive for the good and omit the evil, to seek for that power which strengthens the soul and gives nourishment to the spirit! How essential it is that you should all comprehend that in order to be happy in your future life you must strive to attain individuality in this life. Unless you become individualized in this life you cannot fully enjoy spiritual happiness beyond.

If there be no kind act done to your fellow-man, if there be no good imparted to your suffering brothers and sisters, you can never feel satisfied with yourselves. We find the desire to obtain wealth and position in this life, the desire to supersede each other in material acquisitions, very common. But how little it is understood how it should be applied by those who attain it! They are blessed indeed who attain and apply it to the right purpose, by imparting to the needy, to those who are your inferiors; by feeding the hungered and clothing the naked: those hungry ones who have not been gifted with the power to control the reverses of life, who are at your mercy; and if you have an abundance, it is your duty to share with one and all as far as you can reach them.

Does not the great and good Father impart to the very lowest the same as to the highest form of development? The sun shines with its warming rays upon the evil as well as upon the just. The refreshing rains impart their vapory substances over the just and unjust alike, withholding from none, but all sharing equally in substance. All are children of one great principle, the father of love, the father of justice, the father of charity, and those who err are the weak; they are dependent upon the strong to lead them; and you who are the stronger, who have the intellectual development by which you can lead them, see that ye hold not back, but apply your talents, with all the capacity of your comprehension, to assist them. It is your heaven bound duty, and if you do not realize it here, you certainly will in the higher life; then it will be too late — not too late to make amends, but, disabled as you are, cut loose from the material temple which was of great assistance in your material works, you will find that very little can be done without it. Therefore the return of the spirit, the desire to loosen the shackles which held you to earth.

How is this to be done? You reason with those who are your superiors. They in spirit are not as selfish as you were; they will instruct you, aye, even assist you, by leading you to the shrine, where you will be able to throw off a portion of the burden which depresses the soul. They lead you hither and assist you to accomplish the work you left undone.

Yes, brothers and sisters, in the beautiful spheres of the summer land, there is no selfishness, there is no ingratitude, all, all interblend in harmony, peace, and good will toward each other; and it is the reflections of this beautiful world which casts the rays of spiritual sunlight in your midst, and which is now bringing mortals nearer to the shrine of love and truth.

The spiritual knowledge which belongs to the soul is no belief, but is founded upon actual facts, identical and expressive, and must convince every earnest investigator. It buoys the soul and strengthens the spirit; it invigorates the physical body, the temple of the soul, and gives you power to make a heaven in the material form; it casts off all sorrow and suffering, and endows you with the hope which supersedes all material things; it is the soul-saving power, built on the highest principles, founded on the sublimest facts, and sustained by the all Infinite.

Seek it, O brother! exert your faculties that you may comprehend it, apply it with the right spiritual design, and angel guardians will assist you, stand by you, and protect you through your material works.

From the Medium's Spirit-Brother Jacob. — You in the material form must make conditions for your guides to approach you. Mortals cannot conceive of the good which might be done, if they would comply with the direction of their guides.

I have been very positive with sister Anna the last four months. There were influences that almost consumed her. We certainly have advantages superior to yourselves in perceiving consequences. We study and comprehend the effects upon the nervous system of the medium. We would be more than happy to give you the manifestations you crave with so much spiritual desire; however, the medium must be considered first. Comprehending the effect that a premature demise causes upon the nature of an individual, we have deemed it most prudent to interpose and to guide her into the way, through which her life will be prolonged, and her mission more likely to be fulfilled.

But that link which has united you with our sphere can never be severed. That knowledge which you have obtained has been well applied, and has brought you two spheres higher into the realms of spiritual knowledge; not only yourself, but many immediate friends who have lived on this planet with you. Your controls will say the rest. I will now retire. I must impress the fact that we are ever ready to minister to your advancement, sympathy, and intuitively through the harmonious influence of our medium.

EXTRACT FROM "MILLER'S PSYCHOMETRIC CIRCULAR."

T. You have designated the human spirit as a Christ.

G. The word has two meanings. Christ is an illuminator — a fountain of light and life. Such is the human spirit; such also are those light-giving servants of humanity who, receiving the pure chrisms of interior life, live and suffer to bless the world; and so through him flows life and light to humanity. Jesus, or Joshua, the deliverer, touched all humanity in the divine sympathy of love, a light in darkness dissolving the darkness. What he was all the world of humanity shall be, and greater.

The Christian world pays him divine honors; but remember that a human idea of the infinite is an infinite diversified idea. Let us stand by the black African, bowing to his fetish, holding the largest thought of God he can contain. Look into his spirit. The future angel is there, larger than any material conception of God man has known. He is our brother. Jesus by love and sympathy for man suffered pain and agony, and in that sympathy his love flowed into humanity. He loved, and the world was better for it. He was a morning star of mental liberty.

www.ingramcontent.com/pod-product-compliance
Lightning Source LLC
Chambersburg PA
CBHW020922230426
43666CB00008B/1535